Easily Make People Laugh

How to Build Self-Confidence and Improve Your Humor

By: Dana Williams

ALL RIGHTS RESERVED

No part of this book may be reproduced, stored in a retrieval system, or transmitted in any form or by any means, electronic, mechanical, photocopying, recording, scanning, or otherwise, without the prior written permission of the publisher.

Limit of Liability/Disclaimer of Warranty: the publisher and the author make no representations or warranties with respect to the accuracy or completeness of the contents of this work and specifically disclaim all warranties, including without limitation warranties of fitness for a particular purpose. No warranty may be created or extended by sales or promotional materials. The advice and strategies contained herein may not be suitable for every situation. This work is sold with the understanding that the publisher is not engaged in rendering medical, legal or other professional advice or services. If professional assistance is required, the services of a competent professional person should be sought. Neither the publisher nor the author shall be liable for damages arising therefrom. The fact that an individual, organization or website is referred to in this work as a citation and/or potential source of further information does not mean that the author or the publisher endorses the information the individuals, organization or website may provide or recommendations they/it may make. Further, readers should be aware that websites listed on this work may have changed or disappeared between when this work was written and when it is read.

TABLE OF CONTENTS

PREFACE 4
PART I: CONFIDENCE 1
    CHAPTER ONE: PERCEPTION 9
    CHAPTER TWO: APPLICATION 23
    CHAPTER THREE: EQUIPPING YOURSELF FOR SUCCESS . 35
PART II: HUMOR 1
    CHAPTER FOUR: EXPOSURE 51
    CHAPTER FIVE: MAKING HUMOR YOUR OWN 68
    CHAPTER SIX: PLANNING AHEAD 85
PART III: APPLYING BOTH 1
    CHAPTER SEVEN: THE PURPOSE 95
    CHAPTER EIGHT: AWARENESS 109
    CHAPTER NINE: THE SYMBIOTIC RELATIONSHIP 119
    CHAPTER TEN: WHAT WE LEARNED 128

Preface

Good morning. And in case I've got it wrong: good afternoon, good evening, and good night. This greeting is a spinoff of *The Truman Show*, which was released in 1998 and, although it isn't overt, it was a form of a joke. I'm sure you didn't laugh and that's okay. Truth be told, a lot of my jokes don't land, and I find myself laughing at them more than others do. But contrary to your inevitable first impression, I'm not here to preach about how to make jokes nobody else thinks are funny. I'm here as your advocate, to equip you to utilize humor so you can build your self-confidence, which will eventually contribute to becoming funnier and kickstart a healthy symbiotic relationship. Unfortunately, I can't give you some universal answer to being funny and confident. I can, however, provide you with specific thought experiments and guidance to help you discover how to build self-confidence and improve your humor.

If you're looking for an easy answer, then this isn't for you. The plan is to challenge you to try things that might be new, difficult, and probably a bit silly. The end goal is to awaken a part of you that already exists, because I believe confidence and the ability to be funny lives somewhere deep inside you. Your confidence is undoubtedly inside you screaming, "Kevin!!" Well, probably not Kevin, unless your name is actually Kevin; in which case, how special do you feel? The point is, there is some part of you that's fighting to feel more self-confident, whether it's by using humor or other tools, and that part of you is reading this.

I don't know much about you, but you've already communicated something valuable to me by being here: You want to grow. I'm not sure if your goal is to improve your confidence, your humor, or both, but the fact that you're reading this speaks volumes. Thank you for being here. Hopefully, this is a step forward in being more self-assured. I don't need to be the one to tell you this, but life without charisma is inherently more difficult. Having charisma is like being an extrovert or attractive; the world is simply built for you.

It's one of those things that's hard to measure, but you know the bias is there. There are many studies that support the claim that prettier people receive more positive bias, but there's a finite amount of ways one can thoroughly study the phenomenon, and all too many of those stones are left unturned. Sure, you can list a few perks off the top of your head: "More compelling at job interviews" or "Lively social life" or "Gets more free stuff," but how can we really know the extent of the advantages awarded to those with confidence, humor, attraction, or extraversion? It's the opposite of a microaggression, whatever that would be called. It's millions of subtle cues that are handed out as reinforcements to likeable people.

As a self-aware, average-looking, and moderately introverted person, part of me gets mad at the injustice, you know? Gets me thinking that we should start a petition or riot, or develop our own not-so-micro aggression toward the fortunate. We can identify attractive people fairly easily, with a reasonable enough consensus, and the extraverts speak for themselves, literally. The funnies and the confidents can only hide in the shadows of our oppression for so long. But then it gets messy—who's to say where we draw the line? Would we go so far as to say *I'm* funny? I know many of you wouldn't agree with that, which would work to the benefit of this case. But if it's true, then I'd be the one who picked up the pen and wrote my own deliverance, and that won't fly. Eventually, we'd set up an entire caste system and tier people with ruthless rating scales according to minute differences we wouldn't otherwise notice.

Like many impulse-based, satirically-filled mutiny pitches, this one kind of got out of hand. I suppose reading a book about how to grow personal opportunity is more realistic than starting an uprising, so like I said, I'm glad you're here. On par with most revolutions, this book is intended to help you level the playing field, but it isn't just to feel content when looking over at your peers. On that note: if you're already attractive or extroverted then please move along, we don't need to create more capable human beings. Just kidding, you are more than welcome to stay. In fact, it's encouraged, believe it or not. Even if you have all the magical qualities that previously spurred a discussion of an insurrection, I hope you continue to learn and grow into an even more invincible powerhouse. Which segues into my first point about comparing yourself to others who appear to have x, y, or z desirable traits. One of the most important aspects of confidence is purging yourself from that comparison. Lailah Gifty Akita once said, "There is no need for comparison. Be happy with yourself and find satisfaction in your work." I have no idea who Lailah Gifty Akita is, but it sounds true, right? The Internet also told me that Theodore Roosevelt said, "Comparison is the thief of joy." I have no proof he said that, but he could have. That is the first lesson of the book, so jot that down. "Comparison = bad" should be sufficient for now.

The next lesson is similar to the former so get ready: humor isn't for other people, it's for yourself. I can do my best to teach you how to use humor to build your self-confidence, but it's not reasonable to expect to be able to apply it to everyone. My writing style may or may not be for you, but if I were writing to please you then I'd have nothing to say. I don't know you, Kevin. And that joke may have been the last straw, where you decide you're sick of my bad jokes and opt to stop reading, but I don't care, and that gives me the liberty to continue making stupid jokes that make me happy. There's no series of words you could string together that would inspire everybody to laugh; there's no universal joke or style.

We'll dive into what it means to accept things as they are regarding other people, humor, and your own circumstances. If you want to be funny for your own enjoyment, so you can laugh with and at yourself, then keep reading, my friend, because I've got words for you.

PART I: CONFIDENCE

Chapter One: Perception

You've heard "fake it 'til you make it" countless times, but I'm going to ruin it for you: that's not how it works. Don't get me wrong, going through the motions isn't necessarily a bad idea. Later we'll talk about body language and how simple habits can help trick your brain into feeling more confident, but faking confidence isn't sustainable. Think about it; are you going to fake it on the bad days? Even on the good days, that sounds exhausting. But what about the medium days? Think about last Tuesday; did you feel like faking it at work that day? Unless you had a remarkably good day, the average person would probably answer no. I would.

Confidence shouldn't be a mood that turns on and off like a forgotten blinker in traffic. It's something that should be part of you, like any other trait. It's natural for it to undergo fluctuation but relying solely on a feeling is dangerous and can have the opposite effect. We don't want to cautiously piece together a fleeting thought—we want to erect a sustainable, trustworthy foundation we can depend on. You want to be able to adapt to the ever-changing moods humans inevitably and uncontrollably endure. You can't be expected to fake that on the bad, the medium, or even the good days. You can, however, accept things as they come. You can accept your good, bad, or medium mood; you can accept when you're feeling bloated or bony or boring; you can accept when the job you thought you were a shoo-in for didn't even grant you an interview. Acceptance of the circumstances helps you bear through the hard days, the good days, and everything in between; it equips you with a realism that's necessary to brave life.

Acceptance also applies to specific insecurities, which everybody endures. The person you envy with perfect skin looks longingly at your vivid eyes. Another aphorism I'd like to address is the infamous "it's always greener on the other side" adage. This, of course, is a saying intended to emphasize the importance of perspective. The grass on the other side of the fence looks greener and more luxurious than this stiff, yellow patch I'm grinding through, I should hop over and take advantage. You get to the other side, and it's just as bad as your memory of the original patch, and you look up only to see that your old stomping ground is more vibrant than ever. It would be exhausting and unrealistic to jump back and forth between each side, especially since the other side is often unattainable in real life. People with thin, straight hair tend to desire thick, wavy hair, and vice versa. If you focus your energy on desiring what cannot be changed or pouring yourself into the miniscule things that can be changed, you're going to spend your entire life chasing your tail over an opportunity only you can see.

Don't misunderstand this and think that growth is obsolete because there's always a new issue to face. It is an important part of the process, but growth becomes a chore rather than an ambition when you don't accept where you're currently at. It's not fair to yourself if you decide to love and appreciate yourself only after you've hit your goal weight or once you achieve a certain figure in your checking account. Today is a great day to learn how to accept and love yourself as you are, and from there, we can build on that together. I won't lie and say it isn't difficult to accept yourself or your surroundings, but it is worthwhile.

The locus of control theory offers two beliefs: external and internal. External locus of control suggests you have little-to-no ability to manipulate your environment, and the lack of extrinsic autonomy is the explanation for why things happen to you. If you land a job, it's a series of lucky events that have overlapped in just the right way for you to get an offer. If you total your car, it's due to external factors that were used against you and were out of your control. External locus of control breeds frustration, hopelessness, entitlement, and learned helplessness. It advocates for the belief that you have no say in the matter, no matter what you do. Internal locus of control focuses more on taking responsibility and believing you have control over the things going on. You got that job because you worked hard and are qualified for the position. To be honest, you probably crashed your car into the median because you were distracted by the text you've been waiting for all day.

Realistically, life is a mixture of the two because a lot of things had to sway in your favor to be put in the position to even apply for the job, but you also wouldn't have gotten it without the work you poured into your experience and application. You may have glanced down at your phone when it lit up from the text, but you couldn't have known or predicted there would be a tire in the middle of your lane while you're driving toward it at 75 miles per hour. It's important to acknowledge that, yes, most things that happen are due to a combination of events inside and outside of your control. If you're like me, then you'll pick and choose when to apply them. Of course, it's all external factors when something bad happens, "The tire shouldn't have been in the road as it is, it's the state's duty to get it out of the way, therefore, it's their fault I crashed." Yes, I have actually blamed the state government for debris in the road; that's some mental gymnastics, huh?

Later the same day I could be bragging about all the influence I had in securing a new job, "I'm pretty proficient at résumé-writing, so that didn't hurt my chances, I'm sure."

This type of thinking is based on immaturity, and entitlement and it's something I need to be more aware of proceeding forward. It's natural to want to avoid responsibility and assume others are to blame for occasionally grave mistakes, but that type of thinking devastates your confidence in the long-term and creates a reliance on chance. It's not others' responsibility to nurture confidence within you, it's your own. Developing an internal locus of control and understanding that you have personal jurisdiction is both empowering and humbling. It will also help you become independent, self-motivating, and adaptable. An unwillingness to accept that you're in control is a brash rejection of confidence and it's ill-advised to continue reading if you perceive your own blame as someone else's. As with most things, this is not a universal clause—there are some things that certainly justify blaming someone else—but a good rule of thumb is to accept responsibility like you're hungry for it. Unless that responsibility is for a crime you did not commit; I wouldn't suggest admitting to jail time if you didn't do it.

The loci of control also relate to how you think others view you. The perception of your assumptions toward other people's view of you is referred to as the looking-glass self. An example of the looking-glass self is presuming everybody is looking at you or judging you when you go to the gym. I'd like to think I'm a confident person but going to public gyms tends to shatter that claim. It's hard to think everybody isn't looking at you, especially if you have no idea what you're doing. In reality, nobody cares. Really, truly, everyone else is doing their own thing. I'm projecting my looking-glass self onto a group of people based on my own insecurities. "I don't know what I'm doing, so I'm positive others know I don't know what I'm doing and they're probably watching in anticipation of me doing something stupid." I know I'm not alone in this line of thinking. This perception is a common thought process because, by nature, we want to be a part of the normalized crowd, at least in these cases. Another example can be seen in a reluctance to crack jokes due to the assumption that no one surrounding you thinks you're funny.

Another hard lesson is coming at you fast: you absolutely must assume the best in others' perceptions of you, otherwise you'll be tempted to see the worst because that's what you probably see in yourself. This may not be a difficult concept for you to grasp, but this Clydesdale pill is something I continue to try to wrestle with daily. It's ideal to ignore the little voice in your head that tells you what they might think about you, or to simply be unfazed at their opinions, but that may not be realistic for you. Concern for others' perception of us is something that is socially wired within us. The reason for this is because it's in mankind's best interest to survive together, especially prior to a time when we had incredible technological feats to compensate for our frail, unassuming bodies. Being ostracized by our group could have very well meant death, and it's theorized that we continue to feel the psychological and biological impacts of rejection to this day because of this learned survival skill. This exclusion has been observed in wildlife as well, with animals bearing the social consequences of ostracization, some more gravely than others.

Julia the gorilla, of the Melbourne Zoo, for example, was killed as a result of social behaviors she picked up from chimpanzees in the early stages of her life. Other gorillas noticed some nuanced habits that weren't familiar, and one eventually snapped because of it and brutally attacked her. But there are other consequences of ostracization aside from death, especially since we don't always face those types of natural tribulations as humans in the 21st century. Although, it should be noted that people have certainly been abused because of their differences, notably as a result of sexual orientation, race, disability, fashion, religion, and more. The University of Vienna did a study to observe the social cohesiveness and intelligence of ravens. Ravens are very intelligent creatures, by the way. Seriously, look up "Smartest bird (the intelligent raven solves the puzzle)" on YouTube; it's almost unsettling how smart these birds are. Anyway, a study was conducted to see if researchers could get a group of ravens, which is called an unkindness, to pull a rope and release a cheese reward. Each raven in the group would get one piece of cheese, but researchers found that if one selfish bird ate anything other than their allotted reward, the rest of the group would ignore the other one and refuse to let them participate in future reward-earning challenges.

These stories aren't limited to animals, nor do they only apply to the nonfiction category. We all know fictional stories of social rejection that promoted conformity or utility rather than acceptance or individuality. The ugly duckling wasn't accepted until he matured into an attractive bird. Rudolf the red-nosed reindeer wouldn't have been celebrated if not for his utility in a pinch. For heaven's sake, the lyrics are, "All of the other reindeer used to laugh and call him names," until it was more convenient to have him around, then suddenly the lyrics changed to, "Then how the reindeer loved him." Even in fluffy children's stories we're taught it's better to blend in or, if unrealistic, be better than everyone else by sheer luck.

The point is, we don't like to be excluded and there's plenty of reasons why. Social creatures, like humans, were not meant to live solitary lives so there's a panic feature we all have installed, and we're expected to undergo constant system updates to understand new trends, clothes, entertainment, speech patterns, and more. Even foundational aspects of humanity, such as nuances of morality and styles of humor, come and go with the seasons. It's valid to fear social judgment, but it becomes unhealthy when it prevents you from doing everyday activities.

Trust me, nobody is noticing you. Most people are focused on themselves, just like you are, and it's a good thing. Unless you are doing, saying, or wearing something that blatantly attracts attention, others do not care to be bothered by what you are doing. This includes places such as gyms, grocery stores, department stores, coffee shops, restaurants, or anywhere else that causes you to feel self-conscious. Even if you don't know what you're doing, people don't wait around for fools like you to screw up; chances are, they're there to work out, get food, shop, drink coffee, eat, or do whatever you're doing at the same place. Think back to situations you've taken the time to observe others being clueless. I don't know about you, but that's a thing I've never intentionally done or sought out.

From time to time, I'll indulge in people-watching if I'm waiting for a flight or spacing out at a coffee shop, but I wish I could communicate how little I care about people's busyness around me. I'm sure you're the same way. And if you are looking at others, why? I'd bet it's due to boredom or curiosity. I went through a brief phase where I was intent on becoming more observant. And no, this has *nothing* to do with the fact that I had recently watched Benedict Cumberbatch's

Sherlock Holmes and wanted to be able to deduce basic things about people. It's a completely irrelevant factor that in no way influenced my desire to maximize my deduction abilities. Completely. Irrelevant. I will not be taking questions about the thought process at this time.

Anyway, so I started to notice people, their clothes, their mannerisms, and their accessories, and I did my best to figure out what it all meant. Someone across from me has precisely arranged stickers on their laptop, could that be because they meticulously planned for all of them to work cohesively because they're perfectionistic? Or was it a happy coincidence? I can deduce that the latter seems unlikely given that these stickers are the same distance from one another and appear to compensate evenly for gaps. But it's not enough to categorize this person as a perfectionist simply due to the placement of laptop stickers, so I have to pull from other elements to gather more evidence.

You see? Even though I'm not the one being stared at, I'm definitely the weird one in this scenario. I'm sure you pieced this together based on my rough analysis of the sticker person, but I can't tell you how little I was able to figure out about people. Despite my moderate efforts, this went on for about a week before I lost focus and gave up.

There's also been countless occasions in which I've stared at somebody for far too long because I was unsure whether I knew them or not. And it would be rude if I did recognize them and didn't approach them, would it not? Instead, I broke the social norm of staring at a stranger in order to try to spare another social norm, which was saying hi to someone I knew. I say these examples to provide you with mental cop-outs. If you struggle with people looking at you, may it be true or imaginary, then reframe your perspective to assume the most innocent about the person. Assume they're not staring because they're rude or you look weird; assume they're curious, bored, or simply mistaking you for someone else.

It's hard to be a confident guy or gal if you've got invasive thoughts urging you to focus on others' perceptions and your own negative thoughts. It's all too easy to fall into the gravity of insecurity when you're being excessively self-critical. I think at this point self-reflection is important: if you are hard on yourself, why is that? Maybe you've seen others act flippantly and hurt you or someone you care about as a result. Maybe you fear becoming the people you swore to deviate from, so you work tirelessly to ground yourself, and in the process, you're buried alive by your own hand. Maybe you just hate yourself and look for ways to accept all blame. There are plenty of reasons people aren't confident, but you owe it to yourself to explore why you aren't self-assured and work to unlearn the part of you that believes you're not worth the investment. Like I said in the preface, the part of you that's reading this is fighting for you to be everything you know you can be, and it's the same part that needs to fight to dig up the 'whys' of your insecurities.

Don't let the excuses impede you from gaining control of yourself. Boosting your confidence is not an ego trip, it's another myth that twists your expectations of confidence. Breaking news: confidence and arrogance are not synonyms. Contrary to natural belief, confidence and humility work symbiotically, while insecurity and arrogance do the same. This is why it's important to build confidence as you're constructing a sense of humor; jokes coming from insecurity can quickly turn into bullying, harassment, and abuse. You'll often hear people talking about a bully's self-esteem when considering an explanation for their cruel actions. Self-esteem ebbs its way into crucial aspects of personality, including humor, and can tarnish an otherwise wonderful person. On those days you feel it isn't worth it to fight for yourself, think of those you might hurt when you don't believe in yourself. This shouldn't be the sole motivator, but if you're in a drought and you're the type of person who wants to care for others, then hunker down and write down three things you like about yourself. If you're still stuck, imagine what someone who cares about you would say.

I read a story a while back of a girl who used to be considerably heavy-set. She was sick of how she felt and how people treated her, so she lost a good amount of weight and felt infinitely more confident. Over time, she grew increasingly frustrated that people treated her differently since she shed off weight. She eventually realized people weren't treating her differently because she appeared more classically attractive; people treated her differently because she carried herself with confidence, positivity, and warmth. Others were simply reciprocating the kindness she felt secure enough to freely give. This isn't to say people aren't shallow enough to make snap judgments based on a feature that may or may not be in your control, but those judgments, and possibly those features, are not something you can control. Even if it were something you could "improve" according to society's standards, you don't owe it to anybody to fit within their ideal mold. The intention of this story is not to encourage you to workout, eat healthier, or lose weight. If you want to do all or one of those things because you want to do it for yourself and it'll be a beneficial thing for you overall, then great, go for it. But the lesson here is your perception of yourself, particularly through your looking-glass self, has significant weight. Be wary of your self-perception and don't take yourself for granted.

The secondary lesson is to be wary of how you come off to others. Maybe the reason you're reading this is because you feel like you're a pretty likeable person but can't seem to land any meaningful relationships or connect with strangers. Unfortunately, this ability is incredibly important to being a person in a high-functioning society and lacking this type of charisma can severely impact quality of life. The absolute worst thing you can do while interacting with someone is remain deadpan. People hate this, worse than receiving any type of negative feedback. Not everyone has the knack nor the energy to maintain a seemingly engaged façade, but if you want to walk away feeling like the person connected with you, then caring about what they say and animating yourself accordingly can be a big help. Although I included this bit because it could be valuable to some of you, I add it cautiously, and attach with it the reminder that the focus of this story is to work toward the ability to internalize optimistic aspects about yourself. I'll explain.

Positive thinking is a cornerstone to confidence. It bleeds into how you feel, how you carry yourself, and how to take on unfamiliar situations. Similarly, negative thinking can be a poisonous drug that may feel cathartic in the moment, but it bears prudence of deeply disheartening implications. I'm not saying pessimism is inherently bad. Plenty of pessimism lies in realism and being realistic in discouraging situations can help protect you from hurt. If you apply for a job you're thoroughly qualified for, it isn't pessimistic to take a look at how many candidates applied and how qualified they are to ground your fantasies a bit. Realism is healthy and I'd encourage that habit to continue. I have the utmost respect for those who maintain the burden of hope but recognize despair's reality. Hopefully as we get deeper into positive thinking, the disparity between negativity and realism becomes more evident. But for now, if you struggle with thinking positively then I have a few exercises for you that might help you notice positive things in your life and drown out the unnecessarily negative things.

One simple thing you can do to acknowledge, appreciate, and attract positivity is write down three positive things that happened throughout the day. It may seem unfounded, but humor me. Plus, I don't mean to play this card, but if you're reading this then maybe it's time for a bit of intrepidity. At the end of the day, write in a journal, a sticky note, a blog, or wherever you want, three good things that the day brought. Some days you'll have to spend some time just to even think of one exciting thing that happened in your day but follow through with it consistently and for at least a few weeks.

I've done the "three good things" challenge in the past and there were some days I struggled to come up with the list. Here were some that could be considered otherwise uneventful but made the list anyway: "Told a good pun today," "Got coffee," "Watched a show," "Took a nap," "Didn't work today," "Unexpectedly ran into a friend," and "Ordered a new book." Even if "Got up at the alarm" or "Took a shower today" is the best you've got, then that's still a win. I can't speak for your experience with this exercise, but within a week I started looking for events that could be considered positive. I was seeking out reasons to laugh, enjoy myself, and treat myself. If I was having a bad day, why not buy a donut or order that book I've been wanting? Looking for any excuse to perceive something positive is an excellent foot in the door for positive thinking and enjoying your experience as a human being. Sometimes it's hard to have a good time with the cards we're dealt, but hopefully we can still find some brightness in the midst of it.

Another thing to tackle is complaining. This is a significant one and there's no bigger offender than me. If I'm uncomfortable, upset, or things don't go my way, positive thinking is the last thing bouncing around my head or coming from my mouth. If I'm dealing with discomfort, people know it. However, this can be detrimental to positive thinking. I'm not suggesting you take a bad situation and manipulate the perception of it to an optimistic point of view. That's unrealistic, at least for me. I'm not challenging you to force the good in, I'm challenging you to prevent normalizing the bad. It's also really annoying to be around people who complain all the time, so it works for your benefit and others.

Irritations happen especially in the little things. If I stub my toe, pinch my finger, drop my phone, or anything of the sort, I'll vocalize my frustration. And it's natural to gasp in pain when you stub a toe or pinch a finger, but I allow it to impact my mood. And then I let whoever's around know the inconvenience I had to endure. Anyone else? I focus on the discomfort, unload my grievances to anyone I can, and then carry that with me for hours sometimes. If you limit your complaining you'll produce less bad thoughts, emotions, and behaviors. Have you ever done something you regret because it was one thing after another, and you just snapped? I have. If complaining isn't in the forefront of your mind, I assure you these immature outbursts will noticeably subside in time.

My background is in psychology, which means two things: this book is probably more in depth than you thought you signed up for, and you have to listen to what I say. I'm pretty sure that's how it works. But realistically, there are many things that even I, who studies the impact and influence of the mind, roll my eyes at when being preached "the power of positive thinking." If I'm being offered a supposed solution or exercise for one thing or another, my first reaction is usually exasperation. I say this not to discredit the efficacy of these suggestions, but to validate attitudes about doing a seemingly ludicrous exercise. If this isn't your thought process and what I've advised sounds good to you, then ignore that. If you relate to what I've said and you feel ridiculous at the thought of listing three good things and not complaining, then try it anyway. I now recognize that you may feel silly, but just try it. Two weeks of genuinely trying to write down positive things and avoiding complaints. If you notice absolutely no changes in your thought process, attitude, or feelings, then you can start complaining about lacking self-confidence; maybe shoot me an email if you're angry enough to dig for my address.

Chapter Two: Application

We've covered some basic groundwork for developing confidence, including a few examples and exercises you can try to get you started on the right foot. Now we'll focus on practicing confidence. My high school coach would always say, "Practice doesn't make perfect; if you practice something wrong over and over, you'll know it really well, but it'll be incorrect. Practice makes permanent." Let's practice some confidence, but we're going to shoot for the kind that nurtures your character to be humble and confident, not arrogant, and insecure.

We'll start with basic confidence demeanor. Your body language communicates an absurd amount of information, both to people surrounding you and to yourself. As always, the first step to initiating change is being aware of your starting point. How do you typically act in public and what does your body language actively say about you? Unless you're conscious of your actions, your body language probably reflects your mood, which may not be to your benefit. If you feel self-conscious or unconcerned, your eyes will likely be plastered to the ground or your phone, even if you're on the move. When you're waiting for your take-out meal or your coffee, what are you doing? Personally, I keep myself busy on my phone, like most people, but if you want to be intentional with conveying confidence keep your eyes up and challenge yourself to notice the things around you. What's the ambience of the restaurant or shop? What are people doing? Who comes off as confident and aware, and what about them do you notice differently from others who aren't communicating that message?

Lifting your eyes from the ground is a great way to exude confidence, even if you don't feel it. Eyes are an extremely communicative part of your body, but it isn't the only thing that drives the appearance of certainty. Your posture does similarly. It's natural to slouch when you're sitting, especially for long periods, but keeping your back straight and your shoulders back helps you come off as confident and will eventually make you feel confident. Make sure to keep up awareness so you notice if and when you feel yourself resorting back to your typical stance. If you struggle to maintain a straight back, like most people, you can buy posture correctors to wear around your house. You can also wear it other places if you'd like; my boss's boss used to wear one around the office all the time, so to each their own.

It can be a drag to constantly worry about your posture, and if it's causing anxiety or self-consciousness, it might be beneficial to start the habit at home. Still, eventually it'll become second nature and then you'll accidentally look and feel confident. That's the dream, isn't it? The great thing about these body language tips is that it isn't just for others to know how competent you are, it's to trick your brain into feeling competent, too.

There are additional factors to consider when focusing on confidence in body language. We've covered the two main ones: the importance of your eye level and body orientation. These don't just apply when you're walking down the street or waiting for coffee, they work for conversations too. How do you usually stand and sit in an interview versus with a friend? Where do you look when speaking with someone? My natural gaze goes toward the speaker's mouth, for some reason; I'd like to say it's because I'm trying to read their lips and better understand people, but I really don't think I have an explanation. Maintaining eye contact shows attention and confidence. This is useful for interpersonal, casual conversations with store employees and friends, but it's imperative for job interviews and other professional settings.

Dr. Amy Cuddy is a social psychologist who researches the advantages of powerful body language and its impact on confidence. Her goal is to discover how nonverbal communication impacts how we think and feel about ourselves. Nature is another great representation of the messages body language can offer. Animals that are scared might pull back their ears and put their tail between their legs; we've seen it in dogs, cats, foxes, and more. Birds, spiders, bears, monkeys, and even some frogs are just some animals that alter their body language to appear bigger to ward off threats. There's a reason snakes coil up before they bite; most don't want to waste their energy and venom on things that aren't prey, so they curl up in that signature pose as a warning for the offender to get the heck out of their space. As you can see, nonverbal communication is not recognized and understood solely within human behavior. Animals utilize language to deliver messages to a vast array of other species to communicate content, aggression, fear, and so much more. Bottom line is that body language is important, and as sentient beings, it affects more than just our survival.

Dr. Cuddy discusses the universality of body language and encourages us to expose ourselves to pictures and videos from other cultures. How do individuals outside our own culture react when they're happy, sad, content, fearful, and so forth? The simple answer is that they react the same. People who were born blind smile when they're happy; these aren't taught reactions. Sure, there are some cues we pick up and possibly exacerbate depending on social exposure, but our brain connects with how its body moves, independently of social learning.

Look at the Olympics. People from a variety of cultures express loss, victory, heartbreak, embarrassment, and pride in similar ways. In victory, people display prideful, powerful stances with their bodies open, arms lifted, and chins high. Think of that cliché high school movie or show where the main character gets embarrassed in front of their peers. They make themselves smaller by sinking into their chair, crossing their arms over their chest, and avoiding eye contact. These tells help clue us in to acknowledge how to trick our brain into feeling things we don't yet feel.

One of the most empirically respected interventions in the counseling field is called Cognitive Behavioral Therapy (CBT). I won't bore you with the details of how CBT works and why its efficacy is so high, but its basic theory is that people are controlled by their thoughts (cognition) and these thoughts translate into our feelings and, eventually, our behaviors. Cutting off thoughts at the source and scrutinizing whether they're helpful, true, or irrational will help reframe the brain to fulfill the behavioral goals the client is seeking. Dr. Cuddy and other social psychologists promoting the power of body language are solving this retroactively. Forcing your body to communicate a certain message to your brain will trigger it to feel a certain way to some extent. She suggests that you go so far as to establish what's called "power poses" in circumstances where you might need that extra burst of assurance.

High-power poses are great tools to use when you're feeling inadequate, ill-prepared, or insecure. Dr. Cuddy proposes going into a bathroom before a nerve-racking interview or event and standing starfish-style for a few minutes, this means arms up in a "v" and feet shoulder-width apart. If you feel really nuts, you can try smiling simultaneously. You'll feel ridiculous, it's inevitable, but you've got to trust me (well, the professional). This is science. Research shows your hormone levels in your brain physically change at a rapid pace in just two minutes of these types of poses. Risk tolerance and testosterone increase, while cortisol decreases; the opposite is true for those sustaining low-power poses. It is also advised to practice these types of poses during the actual interview or event, so you can convey power by sitting or standing open-faced with your chin up and eye contact sustained when talking and listening. Body language and other nonverbal communication styles continue to be researched and understood. I encourage you watch Dr. Cuddy's full Ted Talk on YouTube, entitled, "Your body language may shape who you are," and to look more into her research; if you're someone who is fascinated by human behavior then you will enjoy her work.

Another influential study ran by Stanford University's Philip Zimbardo became popularized as the *Stanford Prison Experiment*, in which college students were assigned roles as guards or prisoners in order to study mock authority responses. These assignments were chosen randomly via coin flip, as to not discriminate based on personality, looks, build, or any other feature. Despite the randomness of the role selection, each student began to embody their respective roles to an unexpected degree. These college students acting as guards would treat their peers as insignificant subordinates by addressing them as their inmate numbers, providing punishment through extensive physical activity, removing cell mattresses, being verbally abusive, refusing hygiene practices, and forcing them to undergo embarrassment by removing their clothes. The study ended prematurely due to the guards' infliction of psychological torture against the appointed inmates. It should be noted that the experiment lasted only six days in total. Additionally, more than 50 people witnessed the proceedings to varying extents and only one objected to the moral and ethical unfolding of the study.

Prominent psychological ethics boards arose out of this educational experiment and put measures in place to ensure this experiment, as well as others similar, would not be replicated. Despite the dark turn, the *Stanford Prison Experiment* taught us the weight even fictional roles bear. It communicates the power of believing and internalizing a certain concept, and this disastrous study can be salvaged to society's and the individual's benefit. It reinforces Dr. Cuddy's assertion that assuming high-power poses and perceiving yourself as important will help promote self-confidence. Hopefully, your take of her advice will exclusively apply to your sense of security and not another's psychological torture.

Consistently maintaining these body language tips will reinforce the lesson your brain is trying to learn, which is self-confidence, in this case. Here, I'm trying to encourage you to combat self-doubt from both ends of the CBT theory. We've discussed positive thinking, which is classified as cognitive functioning, and now we've reviewed body language, which is behavior; as well as perceived roles, which is arguably both cognition and behavior. It can be argued that either are effective to advancing self-confidence, but my hope in offering both sides is that you can walk away from this book healthier or more self-assured.

In my experience, it's difficult to build assurance out of nothing. Although I've been discouraging comparison, for good reason, it's not a bad idea to look around and observe others' behaviors. People-watching is a great way to promote awareness and confidence for yourself, and it's also kind of fun. The idea is to notice people's reactions to things and how they interact with people. When you first notice them, do you get a good or bad feeling about them, and why? Usually, we have first impressions for a reason. These initial impressions aren't always right, and presumptions should not be made right off the bat but becoming aware of off-putting features in somebody else can reveal blind spots in yourself.

    I'm not sure if there's an example for my demeanor specifically, but I have found that I can come off distasteful when I'm trying to be friendly and forbidding when I'm not. I tend to weave humor throughout my amicable interactions, which is often encouraged in social situations. The problem is that my natural humor is incredibly dry, so strangers, acquaintances, and even friends aren't always certain of my intentions. A fellow volunteer once made a light-hearted joke about his efforts in folding the pamphlets, which I was to hand out later in the day. I matched his joking nature and said, "Thank you for your sacrifice," with a straight face. In hindsight, even if I appeared to be clearly jesting, that sounded kind of mean. He didn't intend to suggest his service was sacrificial, and my label was clearly an exaggeration of his efforts, making it appear that they were all but useless. At best, it was a bad joke and at worst, I said his work didn't matter, especially in view of my commitment. Not only did it seem that I insulted him, but I also did it in the midst of a friendly conversation, further confusing this poor man. He took it graciously but was certainly left feeling disquieted.

    It wasn't until months later, when I pleaded my friend for an example of my occasional off-putting nature, that he pointed out the uncomfortable interaction I hadn't recognized.

This wasn't a result of people-watching, but it did highlight that even the most aware people, like yours truly, can be quite daft in social situations. Asking trusted friends and family for their take on your interactions with strangers and acquaintances can possibly shed light on things you never would have acknowledged. I look back on that memory and dread the thought of it. I'm sure I'll do that type of bone-headed joke again, but I would hope that next time, I'll at least be conscious of it right after. I'd consider that outcome progress.

Aside from noticing unsocialized behavior, people-watching can also be beneficial for validating habits you thought were otherwise strange. Staring blankly across the room, for instance, is a classic thing most people have caught themselves doing. It's even worse when someone happens to be on the other end of the mishap you just exhibited. The small intricacies and quirks of human behavior are often thought to be weird because you know you do it, but you can't say for sure if others do. You can feel justified in your tiny mannerisms knowing that someone out there is likely mirroring you.

Gather information to make a case on your behalf, to validate your own experiences, grow from your blind spots, and continue in areas you shine. But people-watching doesn't have to be strictly business. I knew a guy in college who would find an outside seat at the top floor of the library just to people-watch. In his case, he wasn't trying to grow himself, he was just waiting for people to fall off their longboard, which apparently, they did frequently in that particular area. Point is, make sure your intent is innocent enough. As someone who has fallen off a longboard myself, I wouldn't want an audience and I'm sure you wouldn't either. And if your intent is a bit malicious, then don't say it was me who gave you the idea.

Watching people fall isn't the only way to have fun and gain confidence. If your goal is to be more engaging, inviting, and part of discussions in small or large groups, but feel like you don't have the social skills to pull it off, then plan ahead. Believe it or not, even extroverts mentally visualize how they hope a conversation or evening will play out. A general tip for life is to avoid being caught off guard. Some people are good at making things up in the moment and creating a memory out of a spontaneous situation, but I'm not like that. For the sake of erring on the side of caution, I'll assume you aren't like that either. If you know you're going to an event, party, gathering, or whatever, come prepared. Even if you don't anticipate attending someplace with a modest or excessive crowd, keeping certain advantages in your back pocket is something you can start to work on now.

Equip yourself with a little piece of something for every scenario. Learn a dance, joke, story, magic trick, talent, song, fun fact, and so forth. For example, if you're at a wedding and your group of friends are like me and don't know how to dance or what to do, then they'll probably be looking for someone to bail them out or distract them. I don't whip this out unless the moment calls for it, but I've memorized a stupid "dance" to break the ice and make people laugh. Your chosen dance doesn't have to be as lame as mine and it doesn't have to be chosen in the hopes that it'll draw focus. You can learn a basic side-to-side and snapping-type dance to help you blend in. I'm going to tell you my signature "move" now, but you can't make fun of me.

Are you familiar with "the jerk"? I'm not talking about "the monkey," the one from the 1960s. I'm referring to the other one, popularized by the New Boyz "You're a Jerk" music video in the late 2000s. It's a really simple move to learn and for some reason it just stuck with me. Just to be clear, I don't do the jerk to impress people, to blend in, or to feel cool, I do it to break the ice. It helps release awkward social tension and unconsciously says to those surrounding, "Yeah, dancing is weird, I'm not sure how to do it normally either." You'd be surprised how many others share your sentiment of feeling uncomfortable during those moments.

Another useful thing to have in your back pocket is a good story. This doesn't have to be something that has happened to you but make it good. Once you think of something compelling, write it down so you can plan the best way to tell it. Sometimes it works best to start at the end: "Oh yeah, my buddy once got detained at the White House on the 4th of July," so the audience is intrigued enough to hear the beginning and middle parts. Sometimes the middle portion of the story can be the bait: "I had a friend who tried to crash two fireworks into each other next to the Washington Monument." Writing it down in advance can also help you figure out zinger lines throughout. There's a reason comedians can take the most seemingly basic story and transform it into a comedy piece—it's because they plan it out. It helps that they're funny too, but we'll get you there. It's also important to note these are people who get paid to be funny, and a lot of them are able to be witty in live time, but every one of them has a script they're hunched over for weeks prior to the gig. Speaking of, you'll want to add a solid, versatile joke to your list of party favors, but we'll review that in more detail in Part II.

Another surprisingly useful skill to have on hand is knowing the full lyrics to a rap song. This sounds less relevant than the other ones, and it is, but it's weirdly empowering to know an entire rap song. It doesn't matter your age or demographic, when you're sitting in a car and *that* song comes on, it's surprising, fun, and a bit comical to bust out the lyrics. Plus, I've genuinely been challenged to sing a full rap song by a friend before. I'm sure it's not a common point of conversation in friend groups, but I'm just trying to pitch ideas and you can keep whatever sticks. Really, any little trick or skill applies to this suggestion. Magic, yo-yoing, skateboarding, drawing, playing a song on an instrument, writing in a fancy font, you name it.

If it's not worth investing time over learning the actual trade, just learn one trick and it'll make you appear far more impressive than you are. And the appearance of impressiveness is essentially the same as being impressive, right? I'm pretty sure that's right. You'll feel good if and when those moments come regardless. And if your casual performance is a success, those are the little memories people tend to tuck away and it helps you develop into a more likeable and fun person in their mind. Maybe you'll write a slam poem and realize that's really your thing and then it's no longer a one hit wonder situation. The only catch is that if you realize some incredible potential or talent, you've got to do two things: 1) publicly appreciate my impact on your life, 2) invite me to cool things. If you're inviting me to something cool, then I might actually respond to that email. Probably.

I know I'm nonchalantly instructing you to become a jack of all trades in order to be more likeable but break it down and prioritize. Fun fact: the saying "jack of all trades" is not the full saying, that's just the first half, it finishes like this: "master of none." So even by becoming a jack of all trades, it's implied you aren't proficient at any of them, which makes the full maxim relevant here. If you think it would be most applicable to come up with a story for any situation, then focus on that. You could even take a well-known, box office story and see if people notice. If someone does notice you're using the plot of *Finding Nemo*, apart from the character names and setting, then you can turn it into a joke if you think you can pull it off. Don't be a deer in the headlights, be prepared for someone to say, "Wait, isn't that just Nemo?" Laugh it off and throw some, "You got me" phrase. However, I encourage you to be cleverer than, "You got me," though, because that definitely sounds like you were trying to lie, and you didn't fool everybody so you're playing it off like it's not a big deal. I just couldn't think of anything better than that, so let me know if you do. You could also make telling known stories your thing. Maybe it's awkward in the moment, but a week later you tell a different story, and that same dude responds, "Hold on, now I know you're just playing back *The Lion King*." Eventually it can develop into a game. That is, until you do have a really epic story one day and nobody believes you because they're busy trying to guess the movie.

    Continue to think of skills that might seem relevant to your interests and circumstances, because each little thing you pick up—reading, juggling, writing, whatever—will reinforce your capabilities and bolster your confidence as we continue to improve your sense of self-worth. Becoming a jack of all trades is more fun than being a master of one anyway.

Chapter Three: Equipping Yourself for Success

Grab a shovel and an order number because you're about to dig deep and be called out. Earlier, I challenged you to ask yourself why you don't feel confident, but this isn't a rhetorical question I want you to brush by. If you say, "Huh, interesting, I don't know," and leave it at that, I'm going to be thoroughly unimpressed. Your goal isn't to impress me, I know, but I am the one writing this book, so that should mean something. Delving deeper into why you feel inadequate is an essential part of growing. If one forces assurance onto someone who doesn't first address their insecurities, they'll probably develop arrogance and an exaggerated sense of self-importance. I'm pretty sure (I'm *hoping*) that isn't your goal. So, I hope your shovel is high-quality because you'll need to hang onto it. This is a long-term process; we're investing in yourself, which means it's worth it.

Settling into your new residence of self-confidence is a trip. You'll need to prepare, pack, motivate, and make arrangements, so you're comfortable. I don't know how you pack when you're moving, but for me, everything is an absolute disaster before anything can get done. Not everyone is like this, I get it, but I reminisce through all my memories and debate whether something is worth keeping, and then end up stalking old friends' social media accounts to see what they've been up to lately. As I said: it's a disaster. This long process is messy and scattered and seems unnecessary, but I'm also one of the most efficient packers I know. Not in terms of time, but space and organization. The investment of making sure I know what I want to do with items and saying goodbye to commemorative trinkets helps the move-in process go much smoother.

I'm not here to try to fix anything, nobody needs fixing. Sometimes they need healing, encouragement, guidance, affirmation, and such, but that's just human nature. This goes back to our previous chapter about acceptance. Sure, we can work to grow our emotional intelligence and tame our feelings a bit so we can act more appropriately in certain moments or meet somebody where they're at in others, but I'm not here to teach that kind of change. Accepting your emotions as they come and learning why you react in a certain way in some situations when you don't in others really helps open the door for growth through self-awareness.

You might be familiar with Maslow's Hierarchy of Needs, which highlight the priorities for physical, psychological, and emotional fulfillment. Of course, you have your basic needs, like food, shelter, and water. The next phase requires general safety and security. Then we graduate to psychological needs, the first of which is a sense of belonging, where you feel love from intimate relationships, platonic or otherwise. The next phase will be more challenging, focusing on your psychological and emotional need for esteem, which involves feeling accomplished and a healthy sense of self-importance. Now we've reached the top, and Maslow glorifies self-actualization, which is gaining access to your full potential. Self-actualization places emphasis on self-awareness, self-discovery, and self-contentment. According to Maslow, most people won't get to this level, despite the pyramid being referred to as the hierarchy of human needs.

Maslow suggests that we need these components to lead a satisfying life. It's not that most people are incapable of getting to self-actualization; it's primarily due to awareness, motivation, and privilege. A significant portion of the Earth's population can't achieve certain phases due to basic resources, like food and shelter. The rest of us probably fall into the awareness and motivation camp. He promoted his model to probably make money as any of us would, yes, but also to educate people on our own capacity and teach us that we can improve our quality of life.

In his lesser-known theory, Maslow's Motivation Model describes the specifics on what is needed versus what will help us grow. "Deficiency needs" are, in order: Physiology needs → Safety needs → Belonging and Love needs → Esteem needs. Contrary to the common belief that confidence isn't a necessity, many psychologists maintain the opinion that esteem is not just an ideal quality to have but a must; it's not a privilege but a right. The goal is not to bore you if you find these concepts underwhelming; the goal is to explain that finding the value that already exists in yourself is justified and worth it.

I hate to be *that* person with a psychology degree but think back to your childhood. Unlike some clinicians, I don't believe everything you struggle with now is rooted in your childhood, but I think you'd be surprised at how many things that don't feel like a big deal have impacted you. I will preface this by acknowledging that having a healthy child-parent dynamic is extraordinarily challenging and I'm not trying to place blame on parents, that is, unless that's what you want. But just because you may have had amazing, loving parents, it doesn't mean you didn't walk away from your youth psychologically unscathed. It's natural to treat your child as someone who doesn't know a thing because they have so much to learn. However, sometimes this type of treatment can be received as chastising, scrutinizing, blaming, and judging. Your parents could have had the best intentions (or not) but still could have unintentionally caused feelings of inadequacy and helplessness. These feelings could have also been fed by harsh teachers, babysitters, or other influential members in your young life.

Whether we have experience with harsh authority figures or not, we all develop some type of an inner critic. This is exasperated with excessive external denunciation and criticism. Sometimes the inner critic is useful because it'll ground you and provide a realistic perspective, but sometimes it's just a jerk and has no productive use. It's important to acknowledge the scope of the inner critic's usefulness because completely demonizing it will probably be more harmful than beneficial. Identifying the difference between advantageous versus destructive thoughts is the key to making your inner critic work for you and developing self-confidence as a result.

In the previous chapter, I touched on Cognitive Behavioral Therapy (CBT) and the impact thoughts have on emotions and behaviors. One of the key interventions of CBT is to recognize irrational thoughts and contest them. If you're thinking, "This is pointless, why am I even trying to read this? It's not going to help, I'm helpless anyway," then that's considered an irrational thought and includes distorted thinking. Distorted thinking refers to types of thought processes that are illogical, often drawing comparisons to well-known fallacies. Some common distortions are catastrophizing, generalization, all-or-nothing thinking, personalization, and jumping to conclusions. The example provided, "It's not going to help, I'm helpless anyway," is an irrational thought based on generalization. In this case, you feel like it's useless even to try, but this logic is only based on a handful of events and doesn't consider other evidence that might suggest you are capable. Acknowledging that some of your inner critic thoughts are really inner stupid thoughts is a decisive step in the right direction. Assuming they didn't laugh at your joke or didn't respond to your text immediately because they don't think you're funny or don't like talking to you is jumping to conclusions. Stop it. Maybe the person didn't process the joke enough to get it, maybe they're distracted because their kid went to the principal's office today, or maybe they just didn't think that particular joke was funny. I could go through likely possibilities for why someone doesn't answer a text right away, but we don't have time for the extensiveness of that list. Use your imagination if it helps but remember the lesson we learned earlier: people think about themselves more than you.

Lack of confidence can apply to a variety of situations: relationships, work, performances, hobbies, and more. Remembering that you have a commitment to yourself and developing confidence is necessary to a self-fulfilling life. I know plenty of people who pour themselves into others and obsess over ensuring others' needs are taken care of so they don't have to focus on themselves. I'm not trying to promote a self-absorbed world, but you need to take care of yourself first, my friend. Are you the type of person who will be the last to eat because you make sure everyone has their food first? If your answer is yes, that's not an innate sign of disregard for yourself, but it might be a clue. There's a very small part of the population who is so incredibly pure that they focus on others first while still loving themselves significantly; the fixation on others' needs is not due to an escape, a fear of silence, self-doubt, or a feeling of unworthiness.

If you are the type of person to set yourself on fire to keep someone else warm, then why do you think that's the case? If any part of you resonates with what I'm saying, then stop reading, ready your shovel, and start to delve into introspection. I can offer you examples of common indications of insecurity until the day I stop making jokes (not going to happen), but it won't mean a thing unless you identify it within yourself first. It may sound cliché, but recording your stream of consciousness into a journal may reveal more than you expect. I'd be lying if I said I didn't do that when I feel overwhelmed or when I can't explain my emotions. And plus, it has become a cliché because it has been shown to be so effective. There's a reason counselors will professionally recommend various forms of journaling.

Most of these suggestions are things you can think about without necessarily doing anything. Even the journaling approach mainly requires thought over action, but what can you *do* to build self-confidence? I've already introduced the idea of having little tricks to equip yourself for random situations, but this time I want to discuss developing a genuine skill. This isn't just a quick cheat sheet of a fact, song, joke, trick, or dance, this is an actual competence in a skill or hobby.

I don't know about you, but just about every single person I've spoken to about adulthood has agreed that it's something everyone is ill-prepared for. I'm not talking about teenagers or college students transitioning into a new life as a young adult, I'm talking about people from all stages of life. As a teenager, you slowly gather your expectations and manage them as you go, but in reality, nothing goes the way you think it does. I think we all get caught up in making plans well into an adulthood that wasn't even close to the actual reality. Goals, values, and priorities change as people get older, and some learn lessons later in life than others. Despite taking life day by day and year by year, life isn't really linear, or at least it doesn't feel that way. We all scatter from one thing to the next until we look up, and nothing's how we thought it would be. I hold the belief that it's the in-between that really makes up our lives and personalities. It's natural to think it's the big decisions, and maybe that is a more accurate theory, but we've still got to bear with ourselves day after day. To me, the days feel slow, but the months go by quickly. What if we found something to make the slow days better?

The older I get, the more I realize the value of hobbies and interests. I recognize not everyone has the time, energy, or means to dedicate themselves to interests, especially balancing work and family. Still, there might be outlets for your hobbies or interests regardless of your busyness. If you commute, listen to a podcast to learn more about your passions; it's refreshing and comforting hearing someone else talk about what you enjoy with the same amount of fervor. You could also pursue more practical interests if you have any. Your spouse may be exasperated if you spend six hours a day playing video games while he or she takes care of the kids, but if you spend a chunk of the day doing handiwork or building a bookshelf, then it's harder to justify complaints about "wasting time." I will say that I'm not discounting the value of video games, you do you, but it was just a common example I've heard can cause tension in relationships. I know there aren't a lot of realistic hobbies that involve being productive, but there's more than you think.

You also may be the kind of person that feels guilty if they're not productive at all times. While that's definitely something you should work out, you could also kill two birds with one stone by picking up a practical hobby. If you are this type of person, I feel obligated to tell you to actually rest and not continue to pour yourself into different types of work but doing both might be a good transition activity for you. I also want to take this time to debunk the common mindset that your hobby, "practical" or not, should become your side hustle, especially if you're good at it. You're welcome to try to accrue a profit out of it if you want but think about the purpose of pursuing that interest in the first place. If you're doing it to unwind a bit, feel more competent in a skill, increase home value, whatever, then maybe placing additional pressure on yourself to perform and meet order needs isn't the healthiest decision. Take it with discretion, you know you best.

What helps you feel confident? Is it working out, dressing to impress, good hygiene, financial stability…? There is a surplus of examples to pull from when searching for a new prowess to make us confident. As I've suggested from my experience, practicing skills that suggest autonomy are great confidence-boosters, such as being efficient in cooking, cleaning, writing, budgeting, and so forth.

I had a friend ask a while back what I would choose to be proficient in if I didn't have to take the time and energy to learn how to do it. I decided I would love to be handy. If something is broken, I want to be able to know how to fix it. If something needs to be updated or built, I want to be the one who can step in and get it done. I don't want to make a career out of it; it would just be a nice skill to have in the toolbox (pun intended). Later that night, I decided to replace some aged, poorly installed light switches and outlets. It took longer than it should have due to the learning curve, and I had to be careful since it was minor electrical work, but I got it done, and now it looks great. If someone were to ask me to for help on theirs, or if it needs to be done for future homes, I can do it, and it feels really good. The simple decision made me feel confident, even if there were growing pains throughout. What makes you feel competent? That's a great step to gaining confidence.

You may even have to force yourself into it. I love writing and editing, but guess how frequently I do it? If you assumed all the time, then you're wrong. This book full of my writing isn't great for my case, but it's true; it's especially difficult to take time to write about my personal passions. I often have to intentionally cut out time and force myself to do the thing I love. It's weird how it works. I have to find the discipline to do the things I enjoy—it's odd. I can't be the only one. If you identify with this, then maybe it's time to set a reminder in your phone right now to encourage you to do what makes you happy. Sharing these intentions with a partner or friend helps bind you to the task; offer accountability for them, too, so you're both tethered to set goals. If you both can't be trusted, then try a third-party source. When I was intent on meeting goals, I would use Stickk, which is a site that commits you to the goals you set for yourself. If you don't meet those goals, then a pre-selected amount of money will be sent to a place of your choosing. Sure, you could pick a charity or friend to donate to if you miss your goal, but nothing is more encouraging than the looming threat of you having to pay an organization you disagree with. Into politics? Commit money to the opposing party if you fail to meet goals. There are other sites you can use, but I found success with Stickk a few years back. It might seem strange to have to strong-arm yourself into doing an activity you enjoy, but speaking from experience, throwing in something new can be hard since it disrupts the normal, drab cycle of the day.

The point of developing a hobby or skill is not only for basic enjoyment but because it reinforces competence. I continue to be brought back to the example of home improvement because I sorely underestimated how empowering it is to fix things. Even if a new thing breaks and you have no idea how to tackle it, having a background of fixing other, irrelevant things solidifies confidence to do the next unknown project. If handiwork isn't for you, there are other options. A friend sought out fighting styles and getting in shape to confirm confidence, and it worked. He pursued Brazilian Jiu-Jitsu and loved the feeling of being able to hold his own. Some form of working out is typically recommended to build confidence for a reason. It fluffs your ego a bit as well, but there is also genuine fulfillment in working hard to look and feel good. Not everyone is in a spot to exercise regularly, so I want to emphasize this is not some sure-fire way you're missing out on if you can't reasonably exercise to any serious capacity. Hopefully, the nuggets of examples are enough to inspire you to think of something that's the best fit for your resources and circumstances.

I'm no hedonist, but my end message here is to do what makes you feel good in the moment. If you're avoiding certain pleasures in order to adhere to certain social or religious rules, then ask yourself why it's important to spare yourself of feeling happiness for the sake of expectations. Sometimes, it's not reasonable to feel a little bit of content when considering what you would have to sacrifice. Contemplate a quick risk-to-reward ratio in your head and, if it's worth it, or if you'd tell your friend to do it, then do it. Some things are happiness investments that offer discomfort first but come with greater rewards later. Long-term happiness investments can be getting your degree, exercising, or even being patient in difficult parts of a worthwhile relationship. Exercise is unique in that it offers long- and short-term benefits. Immediately after a workout, you feel like dying, sure, but in 30 minutes to an hour, you'll probably feel lighter and more accomplished than you had prior to your happiness investment.

Sometimes happiness investments entail managing your burdens and melancholy. I encountered a story about a girl reflecting on her experience in therapy. She was seeing a counselor for her struggle with depression, and the counselor asked her, "What's something you need to get done that feels like it's looming over you?" She said the dishes. They're stacked up high, and her dishwasher isn't very effective, so she has to go through and basically wash each individual dish before putting it in the dishwasher, but she just doesn't have the energy to get it done. "Then run the dishwasher twice," the counselor responded. "Put all the dishes in there, as is, and run it twice. Or three or four times through, however many it takes to get them cleaned." She hadn't even considered that. It felt like breaking the rules somehow, but in this case, the priority was to take care of something discouraging to her and promote mental health with a clean living space.

Sometimes I just don't have the mental, emotional, or physical capacity to cook. There's a voice in my head that says I don't *need* to order in, I have pretty much ready-to-go things here at home. I've got ramen, cereal, frozen food, and so forth, so I can just make that. If I do concede and order food, delivery isn't an option in my head. I always think, "Why deliver when I can just pick up? It's no big deal." And yet, it is a big deal. If I'm dreading a simple activity because I'm depressed, anxious, exhausted, or whatever the reason is, why not spend a few extra bucks to give myself a break?

Treat yourself with the same kindness you would a friend who's struggling. You don't need to be enduring depression to not have the motivation to do things sometimes.

And if you are feeling isolated, regardless of how many people you have surrounding you, there are outlets for you to connect with strangers, acquaintances, and future friends. Find a community that can relate to you, I promise there's a lot out there. There are social media sites, like Reddit or Tumblr, that don't have to be identifying, but can be a point of escape, grounding, and connection. I'm also of the opinion that one should get mental health check-ups just like they would physical check-ups. It is one of healthcare's most daunting tasks to help neutralize the misconception of mental health services only being useful for the severely ill. There's nothing wrong with you for lacking confidence or motivation, that's completely normal, especially living in a culture that thrives off image and comparison. And just to clarify, the thought process that got me here is similar to you getting a bruise and me responding with, "Oh, that reminds me, you need to get your physical soon." Take care of yourself, and remember that there are multiple ways to conserve your health.

  Sometimes it doesn't matter what you do, where you go, or how you get there, as long as you keep moving. What's something you're dreading? As ridiculous as it sounds, completing basic tasks can reinforce a strong foundation for confidence. Being proud of yourself for seemingly everyday tasks is like building your credit. You pay off your mortgage or credit card, and nothing really changes. It's something you don't have to worry about for another month, which is great, but it doesn't feel like some worthwhile investment other than that. But over time, if you keep making these little investments in your credit and yourself, you'll start to see the long-term benefits once you compare your current credit (or self-confidence) to how it was five years ago. Trust the process and know that it has worked for people not so different from yourself.

This is another situation where comparison can be extremely poisonous. If you start comparing your victories to others' supposed victories, you're sure to be disappointed. We all know that one girl from high school who constantly travels for a job she doesn't appear to have, with perfect four-year-old twins and a third on the way, and a beautiful house in the fancy part of your state. All I know is you can't trust the things you hear on Facebook, Instagram, or even real life. Everybody desperately wants to appear as if their life is together for the image of it. It's disheartening because I'm 100% sure everybody feels like they're forced to take on life with faulty brakes while going down the highway at 85, and those people who look like they're enjoying the ride don't exactly help ease your panic. They're panicking, too, I promise. And even if they do have it together, who cares? It doesn't diminish your accomplishments or self-worth.

In accordance with the acceptance aspect I'm continually working to improve, my philosophy is that the amount of pride you feel for an accomplishment should be equivalent to the amount of energy you put into achieving it. I remember when I graduated high school, everybody was congratulating me and explaining how big of a deal it was; there were gifts, a party, and a whole ceremony just to glorify my, and others', accomplishment of graduating high school. As much as I appreciated the intention of well wishes and good goings, I didn't feel I deserved the praise. For some people, graduating high school *is* a big deal, and it should be. The reason I didn't feel particularly proud is because I had all the privileges afforded to me to make this happen. I hardly did homework, I messed around in my classes, I didn't care much about anything, and yet I still passed without a thought. A lot of people do the opposite of my efforts and wind up with far less.

I also played basketball in high school, and that alone awarded me advantages I didn't deserve. I was no star, but a handful of teachers treated me differently because of my activity; I turned in homework late, I was offered grace on my ambiguous exam responses, and teachers were more engaging and friendly with me in class. I also grew up in a very comfortable town where the odds were absurdly in our favor to succeed. I provide this qualifier to acknowledge that graduating high school, whether with a diploma or GED, can absolutely be a significant accomplishment. Even if you had all the allowances I did, you could still be proud to make it through. It's really about your own perception of your experience. I can only share mine because I can't assume yours, you'll have to fill in the blanks for me.

I wasn't too proud of finishing high school, but combatting basic emotions is a significant point of pride for me. I tend to get overwhelmed, and that quickly turns into anger, often to be taken out on people around me. In one instance, I was able to pull myself out of my frustrations long enough to tell a friend it wasn't her fault for my reaction. That seems stupid, but I'm prouder of that moment than I am of graduating high school. Hopefully, that helps illustrate the message I'm working to convey. If you're content with something, even if a friend, co-worker, or family member discredits it, then you should hold onto that feeling of satisfaction. After all, you're the only person who's responsible for your gratification.

I want you to reflect on something you're proud of completing or even starting. I'm the worst at following through with things, but I'm still satisfied with the one song I learned on the piano or the ukulele when it actually held my focus. Make a list of things that other people wouldn't necessarily recognize or appreciate and take the time to feel the pride you deserve for those things. Part of acceptance doesn't only apply to the bad things you can't change, it's necessary for you to acknowledge and accept the good things, too. Acceptance entails working to see the full picture, not a touched-up image someone would post on Instagram, but as the reality of the situation, involving the good, the bad, and the in-between. This recognition is a useful stepping-stone for being content in your humor as well, which we'll slowly discover as we move along and more thoroughly discuss in Part III.

PART II: HUMOR

CHAPTER FOUR: EXPOSURE

We dug pretty deep in the previous chapters, so I'll let you put your spades away for now, but you'll want to hold on to that ticket number because I'm still not shy about calling you out. As with understanding and applying anything else, we've first got to take a look at how humor plays a part in your life. If I'm feeling zesty, we'll even dabble in considering how it plays a part in others' lives because, let's be honest, not everyone was raised the same or had similar tones in their family dynamics. Maybe people's families didn't appreciate, much less acknowledge, humor. That doesn't mean that type of person didn't have fun as a kid, but maybe values other than humor were prioritized. I couldn't tell you why, but when I think of these types of families, I picture a pretentious, well-off British family from the 19th century who scolds their children if a comment is made in jest; they all have some real *Downton Abbey* vibes. I should mention I've never seen *Downton Abbey*, but you get it.

    But anyway, there are modern, less extreme versions of serious families. I come from a fairly somber background myself, but my father often broke that streak with his infamous knack for puns, as dads do. I'm a serious person overall, but I've discovered that maintaining a serious and confident disposition all the time can come off as arrogant, superior, and egotistical. I can't emphasize this enough: don't take yourself too seriously. Even serious people need to take themselves down a peg by laughing at themselves or making a stupid joke; it's a rite of passage for any human being that has their basic needs met. Speaking of which, I'm inclined to repurpose

Maslow's Hierarchy of Needs by adding an elastic clause to the "Esteem" category. To refresh your memory, some of the qualities for this category are respect, self-esteem, accomplishment, and independence, but let's throw in "humor" as well; it'll be our little secret. Abraham Maslow was born in 1908, and I couldn't tell you why, but I imagine everyone born pre-depression lacked comedic ability and recognition. In creating his famous psychological needs pyramid, the poor bloke probably didn't even experience humor in a core way, so he hadn't thought to include it. I'm pretty sure that's ageist, but I'll do some self-discovery or something later to figure out where this assumption comes from. I do want to point out, in case my sarcasm isn't abundantly clear, that I know people had and broadcasted humor back in the day. Notably, William Shakespeare was actually more known for his comedies than tragedies back then, but taught literature has clung more to his morose content than his successful comedy pieces like *Much Ado About Nothing*, *The Tempest*, or *The Taming of the Shrew*.

Time periods, or the presumptions of which, are not the only metric to acknowledge differing applications for humor. Eastern cultures, for example, tend to use humor to illustrate a concept or point, like a fun teaching tool. Using humor to prove a point can be more relevant than you might think. One basic way to achieve this is by drawing silly metaphors to emphasize your point and make the other's point appear absurd in the process. A well-known example of using a joke as a point goes as follows:

A young man was in his freshman year of college. He was anxious to absorb as much information as he could as he sat down for an introduction to philosophy course. The tenured professor dove into the topics of God's existence and encouraged conversation throughout the lecture.

"Well, you see," he said, "Have you ever seen God? Have you physically touched, smelled, or felt Him? So let me ask you: how can you be sure God exists without proof?" A silence fell over the room as his young pupils digested this perspective.

Finally, the eager young man piped up. "Professor," he offered, "I have a question."

"Yes, of course, what is it?" the professor replied.

"Sir, have you ever seen your brain?"

Baffled, he stumbled over his words, "I-uhm-well?"

The student continued, "Have you physically touched, smelled, or felt it? Well, then how can you be sure your brain exists without proof?"

In this scenario, the student used his wit to make the instructor look comically foolish while still communicating his argument. I read this story ages ago, and I'm pretty sure the author of that particular post said the young man was Albert Einstein, but that seems all too convenient to me, so take it as you wish. Regardless, this is a case of using humor to convey a point, especially if the opponent's claim is not very well-founded. This might be a way Eastern cultures communicate this style of humor.

Western humor, however, is more often utilized as a coping mechanism in order to relieve anxiety or stress. Find no further evidence than the distraction of blockbuster movies. How many of them are considered comedies, and how often do non-comedy genre films include distinct bits of humor? It's difficult to make a comparison because Western culture is more saturated with that form of media, but more often, you'll find action, horror, drama, gangster, and science fiction genres more readily than comedy in many Eastern regions.

You don't need to rely on the media to confirm the different uses of humor, just listen to nearby conversations and when people use it. Self-deprecating humor has also been on the rise for the past decade in Western cultures, particularly in America. Hardly a day goes by where I'm not exposed to jokes about depression, anxiety, insecurities, or other grim topics many other people seem to find relatable. Maybe I just need to surround myself with a more optimistic crowd, but it's everywhere I go. It's primarily Millennials and Generation Z who use this type of humor to be relatable, funny, and sometimes self-aware. It could be because I fall into this demographic, but I find these types of jokes hilarious.

I should advise you to be aware of your audience when inspired to make these types of jokes because not everyone will receive them well. And even when they are appropriately timed, the quantity of jokes being spewed is absolutely something to consider, and this goes with any type of joke. Everyone knows a person that tries *too* hard, whether that be at sounding intelligent, funny, confident, kind, and so forth. It's exhausting and, frankly, embarrassing. Don't do this, please. Don't be the person who shoots off too many jokes because one or two of them fell flat or because it didn't fall flat and you're trying to ride the wave; the momentum will subside faster than you'd like if you keep pushing it. Fast-paced bantering is good and encouraged, but that isn't the type of rapid joke-telling I'm talking about—hopefully, you're picking up what I'm putting down. We'll discuss more about what not to do with humor later in this section but notate this valuable bit for now.

Humor isn't solely comprised of punch lines, it's made up of a variety of ingredients. I almost feel too cheesy using this example, but we're running with it anyway; it's not unlike cooking. Maybe I'm the only one who's bombarded by food videos on my social media timelines, but they're everywhere. Sometimes there are the three-ingredient cooking videos, and sometimes it's those overly extravagant Gordon Ramsey videos. Humor can be really, really basic, and it can also be complex with a variety of layers. Insightful, right? You've got to find the appropriate cooking style for you, and hopefully, you'll eventually be able to recognize other, more complex versions, even if you're not proficient in them yourself. A friend of mine would use sarcasm all the time, but whenever I would piggyback onto her joke or continue the bit she initiated, she would respond, "I'm joking." It would be weird because I knew she was joking, considering I was kidding as well, but I think the dryness of my own humor counteracted her version of humor, which was fairly surface level. Well, as surface level as something like sarcasm can be.

It would be unkind for me to suggest that everyone is going to understand, appreciate, and even reciprocate your style of humor. Everyone experiences situations where their joke fell flat to a disastrous degree. Even inconspicuous failures feel somewhat catastrophic. It doesn't seem like it would be a universal struggle, especially when considering charismatic types, but it is. There is an incredibly vast array of humor. I won't even try to cover all of them with you, but here are just a few to help figure out what you identify with most:

DRY HUMOR: I have a plethora of dry humor bottled up inside, but I've learned that not everyone will recognize this form of covert humor. This is the type of humor is delivered in a serious tone or manner as if to suggest you are being serious and not joking. Admittedly, it can occasionally come off as rude, even if you mean it lightheartedly. An important lesson is to be mindful of your audience; I taught you in Part I the only audience that matters is yourself, but I can't necessarily pretend it's exactly the same as it relates to humor. Dry jokes are certainly not outside my repertoire, but I try to be careful how I apply them and with whom. This is my safety style, so it's easy for me to revert to this when I can't think of anything else to offer in a situation, but that's not always good. I hope you remember the story I told you about the volunteer who didn't quite connect with my brash joke about being sacrificial for the cause, which was too dry for the circumstance in hindsight. So yeah, it gets choppy out there.

SATIRE: Like dry humor, satire can easily go unnoticed. Satire is an ironic form of humor, usually to make fun of an existing person or work; a parody, for example, is considered satire. I once wrote a deeply satirical piece about using humor as a cover for true self-deprecation, and my dad approached me to voice his concern about my mental state. While I appreciate his motive, it was frustrating to have something misinterpreted that I was otherwise proud to have written. It comes with the territory, and that's okay.

PUNS: Puns are a form of a play on words and involve using or changing a word to apply to another, irrelevant meaning. A proper response to a pun requires shaking your head and groaning in protest. As a pun lover, even I find myself obligated to this social norm. This reaction is not a disinvitation to stop making these jokes; the same goes for knock-knock jokes, one-liners, and double entendres. These types of jokes are the ones you have to enjoy yourself, so don't expect a standing ovation for them. The riddle that can be answered with this style of humor is this: What gets better the worse it is?

EPIGRAMMATIC: This is wit. If you're reading this as a naturally unwitty person who desires that quality, don't worry; all hope is not lost (probably). Wit can encompass a wide variety of jokes, but important features of this type of comedy include conciseness, relevance, and immediacy. One-liners, double entendres, puns, and more can all be versions of wit. I say that with caution because there are many people who would come for my head if it was known I boldly proclaim puns to be witty, but they are. Don't come after me. Coming to terms that puns are witty is a similar feeling to the infuriating question that no one wants to admit the truthful answer to because it's uncomfortable: Is cereal soup? I feel like, against every bit of instinct in my body, the answer has to be yes, right?

INSIDE JOKES: This is taking an otherwise misplaced concept, word, phrase, or action and making it relevant to others in a humorous way. The U.S. version of *The Office* features the character Michael Scott saying, "I love inside jokes. I'd love to be a part of one someday." Inside jokes don't have to be built from mutual friendship. If you and a stranger or acquaintance quotes Michael Scott and you're familiar with the show, then congratulations, you're a part of a larger inside joke. I'm definitely going to say that example counts. Another easy in with inside jokes is between people who share favorite sports teams. I've had friendly conversations with people for wearing my favorite NFL team apparel more times than I can count, and pretty quickly, we're laughing about how bad our team was last season. I've even had that kind of camaraderie with sports fans from opposing teams; we give each other flack for having the audacity to support *that* team, and we each part ways after a good laugh. Friendly competition is a sure-fire way to get a return on an inside joke you haven't officially established with the person unless the person doesn't care about the team enough or they care too much—then that can get awkward and messy.

LOW-HANGING FRUIT: It's not always bad to go for the obvious jokes; sometimes those are the best. Common low-hanging fruit jokes typically involve stabs at cultural norms, such as gender roles. This is another opportunity to read your intentions and your audience because gender jokes can go from lighthearted to sexist, but if you'd feel comfortable saying it in front of your mother, then go for it. One common play on gender is when the woman is the household's breadwinner while the husband is the stay-at-home dad. This, in and of itself, isn't funny and not abnormal these days, but shows and movies capitalize on this trope by having the other go through the motions of stereotypes associated with the opposite gender. For example, the wife might burst through the door and say, "Honey, I'm home!" and the man is simply glad to see and spend time with his wife. She may also make a promiscuous suggestion to further milk her gender counterpart's typical hackneyed phrase. This type of humor is played over and over again in entertainment, expectedly so.

EMBARRASSMENT: This can be used to ease the tension off an embarrassing thing you or someone else did. It can also be used to exaggerate another person's folly in a teasing way. Be careful using this form because many people do not take embarrassment well, for good reason. This can quickly turn into bullying or harassment, so make sure you know the person you're choosing to poke fun at. A good point of thumb is that if you're unsure, don't say anything. Tip: just because the targeted person is laughing, it does not mean they find it funny or acceptable. I show my affection through these types of jabs all the time, so I'm not discouraging this, but start out slow if you're only somewhat certain and then lay it on thicker as you become more confident in that particular relationship dynamic. I'll go over this a bit more in an example later on.

DARK HUMOR: These are the jokes that would be inappropriate in some contexts and audiences and wildly accepted in others. A morbid joke at a funeral would be a dark joke; they can really be killer sometimes, though. Side note: that last joke was a combination of wordplay, low-hanging fruit, and dark humor, just in case identifying jokes as they come is helpful. Let it be known that this is not my last joke about death, so buckle up, so you don't become the butt of my future jokes. Others might suggest you avoid using this brand of comedy, but I won't. It's easy to use dark humor in bad taste, just as it is for explicit humor, so I'm going to dub this as an advanced or complex form of humor. If you're typically an unfunny person reading this to become funnier, then maybe wade in the water first before diving in the deep end.

CULTURALLY RELEVANT JOKES: This is another category that umbrellas over an assortment of jokes. For example, if a celebrity couple famously gets a divorce, you might use their name as a verb in irrelevant, nonchalant situations: "Sorry you guys, I've got to Kardashian out. I have a paper due Sunday, and I can't miss the deadline again." Not the best example, but you get it. An example can be looked at within CBS's *How I Met Your Mother*, where the main character, Ted Mosby, gets left at the altar on his wedding day. Later in the show, the audience discovers that his friend Barney, who is an infamous flirt, used a pick-up move called "The Mosby," where he approaches an attractive stranger at the bar and confesses that he recently got left at the altar to gather sympathy points, which convinces her to go home with him. This isn't culturally relevant as much as it's contextually relevant, but they're both stitches from the same quilt.

MISDIRECTION: The best way to pull off these jokes, in my experience, is to add detail. The more detailed the scenario you're painting, the more believable it becomes for the audience. As you build up and the misdirection comes, it almost feels like it was a surprise, no matter the anticipation of the joke or the tone of the story. Misdirection can also be as basic as using unpredictable adjectives to describe common situations or answers. For example, when the question of my height comes up, I will tell people I'm a crisp 5'3". I'm not sure why, but that answer makes sense in my mind, and hearing something like height being described as crisp is a little out of left field, so it's subtle yet a bit unexpected. You're welcome to steal that. In my opinion, that adjective fits for all heights, but feel free to use comparably funny alternatives.

EXAGGERATION: This is a great tool to use in funny stories, and, just like in misdirection, you want to make sure it is rich with detail. If you describe your third-grade teacher as someone whose skin is chipping to reveal the true, green nature underneath, that's a much better way of communicating that you think she's a witch. The devil's in the details, my friends. As you're learning, there are many examples of these styles overlapping because humor is such a dynamic form of communication. On a bolder day, I might even consider this a lightly elegant form of figurative language, but it depends on the joke. Hardly a joke goes by without the assist of exaggeration; it's not exactly used sparingly in this craft, for good reason.

EXPLICIT: These types of jokes are often sexual in nature, but it can apply to any form of breaking socially acceptable topics, such as including an uncomfortable number of details regarding a violent act or grotesque autopsy. This can easily overlap with low-hanging fruit, dark humor, epigrammatic, and more. This is a wide scope of humor, but I decided to include it in this list to offer a friendly notice that using explicit jokes can be an easy way to get your foot in the door of humor. It can also make you come off quite poorly if you don't use it correctly, so feel the room. To recap: it's low-hanging fruit but can be high risk if applied improperly. People typically appreciate this one because it's fun to engage in socially taboo discussions and laugh at inappropriate jokes. This is a natural form of control that people enjoy feeling and sharing.

These are all useful forms you should familiarize yourself with, but the type of joke isn't the most foundational aspect of humor. You've probably already heard of the stress people place on the delivery of jokes. The reason this is such a substantial component of humor is because delivery can make the blandest responses comedic. You know those people that are just funny? They don't necessarily tell jokes all the time, but there's something about their mannerisms or witty responses that bust you up laughing almost every time. I'll tell you right now I can't teach you that type of humor; I'm very sorry. If you're reading this in an effort to become that person, then please provide the courtesy of letting me know when you start the support group so I can join. Let's just say you would never want to go on a double or group date with this person because they'll make everyone else look like de-shelled tortoises. But anyway, enough envying other people living our dream, this person is probably funny because of their delivery. I guarantee it. Imagine that person saying something that would get a laugh, and now imagine yourself saying the same thing. Delivery.

So how can we work on building your delivery to genuinely improve your humor? One powerful tool of comedy that relates to delivery is timing. Sounds familiar, right? I'll pretend to be surprised you've heard of comedic timing. This can apply on either end of the time scale, meaning there are appropriate moments to use a faster or slower delivery model. For example, a common joke that reflects the former model goes like this:

"Hey, Stan. What would you say is the most important part of humor?" Luis asked.

"Uhh, I'm not sure, I—"

"Timing."

This joke has been told and re-told, so this isn't original content by any means, but if you deliver this joke to a person who isn't familiar with it, it's funny. Here you're setting up the joke, which is kind of meta because you're talking about the topic of humor and executing the punchline in a way that surprises the audience and reinforces the answer by emphasizing the point. It's a bit of a fun one and easy to pull off. Is your dad cliché like mine, in the sense of appreciating "dad jokes," like a play on words? If so, try this with him, or really any dad. I'm going to say you've still got a decent shot of making the person laugh, even if it's with a dad who's a stranger.

Interrupting people for a joke can get old quickly, so it's for the best if you don't interpret a faster delivery to mean immediate unless the joke calls for it like the last one. Talk briskly through the nuances of a joke, such as the details that make it appear more vivid and set your audience up for a harder crash at the punchline. This makes you appear confident in your joke, and, hopefully, it will distract people from the fact that you're setting up a punchline; no guarantees, but it also might make you appear smarter, so that's a plus. Unexpected punchlines are the ideal set-up for funny people; it's equivalent to magicians performing for children or drunk people—these situations are groomed for the maximum effect. Quick details are also a way to prevent your audience from guessing the joke prematurely. If you're depicting a situation and something's out of place, you might not want them to notice it just yet.

For example, every now and then, I'll tell this story about a trip I went on in college; it's nothing too extravagant or funny, but my life is boring enough that I find this relevant to bring up every other year or so. To start, I always give an appropriate background to let the audience know what to expect or to emphasize a particular part I want people to remember. In this case, I want you to know that I'm the type of person who waits until the very last moment to pack. I'd consider it a tradition, but I'm the only one who partakes in it, so it's really just my personal tradition that family members disapprove of. Anyway, I'm about to go on a trip but I wait until *the* last minute to concern myself with packing. Naturally, it's the midnight before my trip and I have not yet packed a thing, per my customs. Instead, I decide to hang out with a friend, because I was in college and apparently allergic to sleep. I hung out with him for a bit and then left at 2 a.m. or so. I'm a bit tired, but not excessively, so I arrive home, throw my clothes in the washer, and decide to take a quick nap. Oh, did I mention my phone was broken? Five hours later, I've apparently missed several calls from the people I was supposed to meet 15 minutes prior. They were calling to ask where I was since we should've already left by then. Let me ease a little tension for my readers: this was a road trip, so no planes were missed in the making of this story. I pop up, panic, and start to pack like the champion I am. But of course, I threw my clothes in the washing machine before I crashed for a "nap," and that was pretty much all the clothes I needed. I threw my clothes, wet, into my suitcase and bolted out the door.

  My misery and, frankly, stupidity in that situation is what makes it funny, at least in my opinion. The fact that I was late and my phone was broken were great contributors, but the sopping clothes were really the cherry on top. When I tell this story in person, I make sure to mention the laundry detail casually and in the midst of a series of other actions so it doesn't appear like it will be relevant later on. If I awarded a pause or even a full fragment of a sentence to the washing machine part alone, people might pick up on where I'm going with it as soon as I mention my falling asleep. This story may not be the most hilarious, but hopefully, this illustrates why it's important to speed up and add detail every now and then when telling a story with any sort of punchline. Also, make sure to grimace in all the right parts if you're telling an unfortunate story about your own misgivings. That way, you can bag sympathy and laughter in one gig. You're welcome.

On the other end, you can slow down your delivery, sometimes to the point of taking extended pauses. It can be daunting to use silence as part of your delivery, especially if you're with a group of friends and you're afraid they might interrupt you before getting to the punchline, but if you're comfortable playing with silence in the midst of an otherwise un-funny answer, then you might just become a funny person. This is something you can apply in everyday conversations, but remember, over-use is your enemy, just like anything else when used in excess. For example, someone can ask you how old you are, and you can take your time before responding, "I'm going to say 38," as if you're not completely sure of your own age or as if you're suggesting that it may not be the true answer when you are, in fact, that age.

Figuring out your own voice takes practice, which we'll review next chapter, but for now, I'm going to give you a couple of prompts communicated in the style of an imaginary game show to test you on your timing. You will guess whether the punchline should be delivered quickly or slowly. Of course, this is a book, so I'm going to need you to really apply yourself and visualize a nationwide audience as we delve into some of these situations. Alright, are you ready? Great, let's play "Bide Your Time or On The Dime."

Your first scenario: someone asks you, "Who's your favorite superhero?" You decide to avoid the typical answers, such as Batman or Spider-Man, and make it into a joke, so you say, "Vanilla Ice." For maximum funniness, would you bide your time or say it on the dime?

Next one. You're asked for a joke on command, you panic and go with the first thing that comes to your head: "What do you call it when Batman ditches church? Christian Bale." You know how this game goes: do you Bide. Your. Time. or say it On. The. Dime.? For my own well-being, please picture an audience chanting the name as if we were attending a beloved game show. If you didn't read it the correct way the first time around, please go back and read it with gusto to truly immerse yourself in the experience. Thank you.

For the prompts above, I'd personally recommend saying the punchline quickly in the first example and take a pause in the second. My reasoning for the former is because you want to encourage others' assumption that you had the obscure, not-so-relevant answer of "Vanilla Ice" on hand and were waiting for the opportunity to provide the answer to this specific question. It's also funny because he's an outdated rapper you probably haven't thought about for at least a decade, and this is aside from the fact that he is thoroughly and irrefutably not a superhero. I'd pause for the second one because you want the audience to process the question before giving them the answer. This is slightly riskier because if someone already knows the answer, they might blurt it out and ruin your moment, but waiting a moment builds up the suspense for people who haven't heard it before. But really, the ball is in your court. Play around with it and figure out your audience. As always, even if people don't laugh, try your best to have a good time. In all honestly, most people end up laughing at how funny I think I am rather than my actual joke.

I provided these scenarios with answers in mind, but my humor is not yours. In fact, a linguist from Texas A&M decided to study a phenomenon that everybody seems to recognize as important, even though people are unable to define it or assign specific rules for when to properly apply it. Comedic timing is important, as we've seen in our own lives and from professional funny people (also colloquially referred to as "comedians"), and this researcher wanted to quantify it. The results suggest that it isn't possible to ground this ability in an explicable way. The very same joke would be told with a pause before the punch line with one audience and get a massive laugh, and the next night it would be told without a pause, and it would receive a laugh just as big. Audience reaction is everything, on a stage and in real life, so the message is that it's different per person, scenario, and audience. Basically, there's no science to this, you pretty much wing it and hope for the best—is that helpful?

This chapter outlined a brief introduction to the many varieties and styles of humor. It wouldn't hurt to continue research on styles, examples, and applications to further enhance your understanding of humor, when to use it, and what style fits you best. In the next chapter, we'll discuss making humor your own by finding what styles best suit you.

Chapter Five: Making Humor Your Own

Let me start off by clarifying that most people aren't original. I steal jokes all the time. In fact, most of the humor I communicate through written means rather than in-person bantering is taken from jokes I've heard in the past. If you feel weird or guilty stealing jokes, then have the peace of mind that even professional comedians inspire their content with other people's jokes, stories, and ideas. If there's a particular joke you feel guilty delivering because it's just too good not to give credit where it's due, then feel free to cite your sources. For jokes like the Batman/Christian Bale one? I'll be honest, I didn't invent it, and I'm not going to take the time to dig up the person who did. At this point, it's been excessively circulated to the point that pinning down the true author is very likely impossible.

If you can come up with your own stuff, then that's amazing; keep it up. You probably shouldn't be reading this if you write all your own jokes because you've obviously surpassed me; coming up with original funny content is *hard*, especially one-liners or similar types of jokes. The only original work I've got is witty banter, and I can't exactly include that on my friendship application's cover letter because that sounds either fake or braggy. Tuck all this away in your head to reaffirm that you're not the only unfunny person without original ideas because that's all of us. Like I said earlier, the thing that makes a joke funny is the delivery, anyway—that's the real talent. If you've got that part down, it's your joke as far as I'm concerned.

There are also a few cop-outs you can use. Credit goes to Vanessa Van Edwards for some of these, as she wrote an article on specific ways to be funny, and I pulled a couple of examples from it; you should check out the full article. But remember how we talked about misdirection and exaggeration when we broke down the different types of humor? Well, here's a few explicit ways you can apply them. Surprising your audience with humor can be simple if you say the opposite of what's expected and/or be oddly specific. Saying the opposite of what's expected can include saying "yes" to questions you'd answer "no" to, or vice versa. Simple enough.

Let's say you were a massive fan of a rock band when you were a teenager. Everything was Green Day themed; you had clothing, posters, tickets, every album, and all the merchandise you could handle. Years later, you're moving, and your roommate spots a box containing a disproportionate amount of Green Day paraphernalia.

"Big fan of Green Day, eh?"

"Nah."

Obviously, you're kidding in this scenario because you have a crate full of once-prized Green Day attire, but it's an easy way to offer a funny quip about your now-comically intense rock band phase. Or perhaps you're talking with someone you don't know very well, and they have a tendency to ask irrelevant, personal questions you'd prefer not to indulge by providing them genuine answers. You can respond in a way that addresses their question, as not to be rude but avoid the answer completely.

"How many siblings do you have?"

"Hmm, that's a toughie. 'Cause technically, my mother and I usually have different answers. It probably has something to do with the fact that I include a running tally of all the pets we've ever had, so it's hard to say."

This dodges the question but gives you a light-hearted response that might get a laugh rather than the awkward silence you'd probably get if you simply said you weren't comfortable answering. You could even take it in different directions, depending on your mood, the situation, or your type of humor. Let's say their response to your answer is: "Give me your best guess."

"Hmm, somewhere between 2 and 8."

"Okay, so your mom would say 2, it sounds like. You have 2 siblings."

"I wouldn't say that either; are we counting dead ones too?"

And there we have dark humor. I have a good friend whose mom, unfortunately, passed away several years ago, and she makes dead mom jokes around people she trusts all the time. Granted, she limits this type of humor to people she knows won't get offended, but even as a pretty unoffendable person, the jokes can be jarring when I'm not ready for them (which is always). It's not everyone's cup of tea, but there are opportunities. Even if you don't have any deceased siblings, answering in this way will likely shut down this conversation. It could also make the situation awkward, but depending on who else you're with, and if you're at wit's end with this person's invasiveness, it might be an appropriate response. Or you could've stopped it before it got dark by responding to the question even more vaguely: "Hmm, somewhere between 0 and 1,000, that help?" The response finishes with a closed-ended question, and it communicates your unwillingness, or lack of desire, to engage in the dialogue further. It also transitions the conversation to a more light-hearted, sarcastic note, rather than ending it by simply saying, "Bug off." Being vague and not answering a direct question should, ideally, be an answer enough. And when it's not, that's on you.

Along the same lines as the previous example, following the logic of withholding, my dad would advise you to never disclose your expected salary in a job interview. If the question should arise throughout the interview process, don't give a straight answer. If they insist you figure a figure, he'd tell you to say, "A million dollars," so you can respond to the question but avoid the answer. This can ease the natural tension of interviews and present personality, which is direly needed in professional interviews, believe it or not. While I think that response is funny, I think it can be better, which introduces us to the specificity of numbers and how it adds to the joke.

When answering the salary question in an interview, I would say something like, "$2.82 million," if I were following my dad's advice. I think it's funnier because of its specificity, but you do what you think is best. You know my usual shtick of saying that I'm a crisp 5'3" when talking about my height? Apply that type of abnormal adjectives to basic responses, even in said job interview. "A modest $2.82 million," or "An agreeable $2.82 million," or "A spunky $2.82 million." Okay, that last one was pretty silly, but maybe you're the type of person to go for that one; if you like the silly one but feel it's a bit too much, try "lively" instead, it has the same message, but feels more professional. Or you can add definitive words for situations that are clearly ironic or ambiguous: "$2.82 million. Minimum," "$2.82 million or I walk," "I've got another offer for $2.82 million at [competitor company], but I'm open to negotiating." Of course, this is a professional job interview, so take these with a grain of salt. However, in my experience, showing personality in the interview process helps you stand out and cuts the room's tension. I feel I'm on the verge of overusing the salary question example, but hopefully, by adapting and expanding it as I did, it showed the potential for other, unrelated jokes.

Another way to apply humor is by switching the expected narrative. For example, I know my mom isn't the only one who orders drinks and says, "Aren't you going to card me?" when the waiter asks my sister and I for identification. This is particularly funny because my mom has gorgeous silver hair, which makes it abundantly clear she's not young enough to be sub-21 years of age. Granted, she says this every time we order alcoholic drinks, so I'd say that's overdoing it a bit, but she's demonstrating how to switch the narrative. She cuts the mundane situation with humor, which is unexpected; the precedence is also set for my sister and I, who look younger than we are, to be carded, but the narrative is shifted when my mom includes herself in an otherwise exclusive circumstance. This also gives the other party the opportunity to compliment my mom for how youthful she looks despite her having two adult children. It's a multi-faceted scheme.

Humor can also be used when telling a basic story that doesn't include anything inherently funny. The difference lies in delivering it suggestively as if something funny or exciting is going to happen, but it never arrives. You can tell a story, say, of you getting coffee, and be specific about strange things, so it implies significance. And when you finish, you'll be asked follow-up questions about the remainder of the story, and the realization of the absence of relevance will set in. I'm not sure if I've seen this described somewhere, so there could be an actual term for this, but I think I'll call it "anti-climactic onset" for now. I feel like that term doesn't exactly make sense, but it sounds good to me, so I'm keeping it. And plus, by all accounts, I've dubbed this a unique style of humor, which gives me the rights to name it. It sounds good, though, right? Yeah, don't answer that. But in my mind, anti-climactic onset plays out something like this:

"You guys wanna hear something that happened today?"

"Oh yeah, sure."

"Okay, so it was technically in the coffee shop, but I think I need to start before then. It took me like eight minutes to find a parking spot, which was honestly fitting for the day I was having, and when I finally parked, there was a huge, red truck parked across from me. It was barely parked in the lines, it was so huge, and my bumper was about four inches away from it. I go into [cliché coffee shop name], and I get in line. Five or so minutes go by, and I'm ordering at the register, and I guess the girl taking my order's name is Vanessa. So Vanessa enters the information into the system for my medium iced Americano with two pumps cane sugar, and a dash of cream. I pay with cash this time, even though I normally pay card, which was kinda weird. Vanessa's getting my change, right? I take it and stand by the bar and wait for my coffee. There are no less than six tables around me, and all of them are full, so I kinda kept shifting in place as I waited for my coffee. I'm not the only one who hates that, right? And then, it finally happened. They called my order, I grabbed it, and left."

Inevitable silence while they expectantly wait for the rest of my experience.

"Okay, then what?"

"Then I came here."

"Oh, that's it?"

"Yep."

And then I imagine they laugh because of their sabotaged expectations. It was either funnier in my head and/or it didn't translate on the page that well, but sometimes setting up the story to be a joke and letting the audience realize the fact that there is no joke *is* the joke. It's hard to say in a fake scenario, but I'd probably label this as a form of dry humor. Explaining a story with dry humor is just intensely difficult, so give me a break here. I'm more of the in-the-moment funny kind of person, as I've told you, so writing examples isn't as much my forte as is my impeccable wit, but I hope you bear with me and can think of how you would apply this type of humor regardless of my poor example.

Despite the examples I've provided over the course of this chapter of how to intentionally and specifically introduce humor to certain situations, I want to remind you that you still do not need to create original material. I highly encourage you to intentionally seek out people you find funny so you can continue building a mental portfolio to use in real life. Maybe you can pinpoint *why* that annoyingly funny person is so funny. What about their delivery or content makes people laugh? Do people around them laugh because it's out of pity, discomfort, or even malice? Hopefully they're not just laughing at the person, but hey, I can't discount that possibility.

Your observations don't have to be focused on your personal life, look up comedians of all sorts. Parodies, stand-up, television, comics, or whatever else you personally find funny, are all valuable assets for you as you find your own comedic voice. If you need a bit of guidance on where to start, we can go over a few popular recommendations. One of the most animated comedians of all time was Robin Williams; a lot of people were able to relate to his variety of comedy. John Mulaney is another popular American comedian; his shows are currently featured on Netflix if you're interested in his work. Jim Carrey may not be your preferred style of humor, but man that guy is a funny dude. He ranges from stupid, slapstick humor like in *Dumb and Dumber* and *The Mask* to a more dry, morose humor in *A Series of Unfortunate Events*, as well as everything in between. Steve Martin, Dave Chappelle, and Jerry Seinfeld are all classic comedians with a variety of styles. I'd also recommend skits from Keegan-Michael Key and Jordan Peele as well. Those guys are insanely talented, and a lot of their stuff is pretty funny in my book. Last I checked, their skits can be viewed on YouTube and Hulu. Some of my favorites from Key and Peele on YouTube are "Two Church Ladies vs Satan," "I Said Bitch," "Substitute Teacher" (a classic), "Al Qaeda Meeting," "Awesome Hitler Story," and "White Zombies." As you can probably tell from the titles, they tend to have darker humor. If that's your style, you can specifically look into comedians with dark senses of humor, like Daniel Tosh, Bill Burr, Bo Burnham, and Ricky Gervais.

You can also look up SNL's most famous skits. SNL skits are pretty hit or miss in my opinion, but some of my favorite ones are: "Close Encounter," "Teacher Trial," "Star Wars: Undercover Boss," "Black Jeopardy with Chadwick Boseman," and "Meet Your Second Wife." Not everybody's taste aligns with mine and that's totally fine, if not wholeheartedly encouraged; but I figured I'd throw out some suggestions of well-known and appreciated comedians, as well as specific videos I've enjoyed, to help get the ball rolling. If someone came up to me and said, "You should really watch comedy more often," I know I wouldn't know where to start. Hopefully this helps. And if you decide my opinion is awful, then that's one less version of humor you know you relate with. Thomas Edison famously said, "I have not failed, I've just found 10,000 ways that won't work." I do not wish for you to go through 10,000 videos before discovering your preference, but hey, progress is progress.

You can also ask friends who their favorite comedians are and inquire as to why they think they're funny. They may not know the answer right away, but it's okay to put a pin in it and ask later. I'd consider this process a happiness investment, one that rewards both you and others. This option might be better suited for you instead of taking my suggestions because it's far more likely you'll agree with your friends' opinions on what they think is funny rather than mine. But, if you think they're idiots who are just fun to be around or just plainly nice, then go with mine to start off. The gist is: look for humor everywhere you go. Studies suggest that people who find amusement in their daily life use and appreciate humor more frequently. Like referenced in Part I, positive thinking and comedic association is an opportunity for your brain to open up to that type of exposure.

The reason this is so effective is due to neuroplasticity. It's a cognitive neuroscientific term that refers to the adaptivity of your brain; it can also explain the development of habits and addictions. Neuroplasticity is when neuropathways are established for new experiences and it will continue to be reinforced with repeated occurrences. Nobody taught me the following comparison, but it has helped me understand the concept more. I've always visualized a large, wooden board as our brain's circuitry. In this board, there are hundreds of tiny divots and lanes. Realistically, there are trillions of neuropathways in your brain, but I figured it would be simpler to picture hundreds of pathways instead. This board is at a slight angle, and marbles, which represent thoughts and behaviors, randomly roll down the board. As neuroplasticity begins to take shape, these indented avenues become more prominent, making it easier for the marble to follow that path; it's as if a carving tool emphasized a particular part of the board in order to get the marble where it needs to be. This has always helped me solidify the idea of neuroplasticity because I can visualize the divot edging deeper and deeper as I make each decision regarding that habit. The purpose of describing neuroplasticity is to illustrate that you can physically change the chemistry of your brain as you make choices. It often feels like you can't control your thoughts or feelings, but in reality, you're more in charge than you think. Positive thinking matters.

As you know, people watching is always a great opportunity to pick up on cues people give off when they make others laugh. In case I haven't iterated this already: I want to mention that the point of becoming funny is not just to make other people laugh, it's really for your own enjoyment. I'll bring this up several times, I'm sure, so feel free to notate this little tidbit now. However, I acknowledge that making people laugh feels good, helps you become more likeable, reinforces your humor, and helps you understand if your humor is appropriate for the mood. It's certainly not a bad thing to feel good when making people laugh. There are many things I advise against when learning and applying humor, and others' reactions will help you gauge whether your joke is within the realm of acceptability in that particular group.

Before diving in on what not to do with humor, it's necessary to say that inappropriate humor might be admissible if the joke outweighs its offensiveness. Take that with a grain of salt because what's funny to one group may be offensive to another. That clause is not a universal rule, so just use your very best judgment and be aware of how your humor might impact someone else. I'm sure many of you want to skip the next part because it will be about precautions, warnings, and misuses of humor, and you're welcome to do so, but chances are, the ones skipping it are probably the people who need to hear it the most. Without further ado, the first don't in the category of humor: do not use humor as a means of harassment or bullying. I hope this goes without saying, but it happens all the time and I feel it's very necessary to mention. I think everyone's been a victim of someone else's joke that was possibly well-meaning, but it ended up being more hurtful than anything. Even if it's "no big deal," you don't want to be the type of person who inflicts harm on someone else just for the potential of a three-second high you might get as a result of people's laughter. You can't possibly be weary and considerate of every single person in every single situation, but at the very least, try to consider the impact your joke might have on those around you. This should be especially easy to do, should you take my advice on planning your joke, which will be discussed in Chapter Six. And if you do joke to jab at someone playfully, make sure they can take it and, for your own benefit, make sure you can take it back. But also, you're going to mess up. I want to acknowledge that right now. I'm mainly talking about people who are careless with what they say and then surprised when things blow up. I've said many hurtful things that were meant to be funny in my time and I'll inevitably make accidental hurtful jokes in the future, too. Take ownership and heed the lesson for the future.

  Another thing to consider is don't dish it if you can't take it. I'm sorry, I don't make the rules. There are certain nonverbal understandings when it comes to humor, especially when involving different types. If you opt to go with a more "prodding" type of humor, where you give friends a hard time for something they did that was embarrassing or just plain stupid, then you have to feel comfortable accepting returns when you inevitably do something stupid or embarrassing. It's okay to joke around with your friends—I'm not trying to be stiff in this context—but your street cred won't die if you pull someone aside and check to make sure that type of jiving is okay with them. Don't assume.

In fact, sometimes it's your obligation as a dutiful friend to give someone a hard time for doing something rude, stupid, or accidental. Something that comes to mind is from NBC's American version of *The Office*. And no, I won't stop quoting popular culture, especially this particular show. If you're not familiar, it features a great episode about the power and applicability of humor. The episode includes characters Michael, a well-meaning boss who misses the target of humor for every shot he takes, and Jim, who is more relatable to the audience due to his on-brand jokes and second-hand embarrassment of Michael. They both return from a business meeting with Michael soaking wet and, it is discovered that he embarrassingly fell into a koi pond at the site. In this episode, Jim feels guilty because he could have prevented Michael from falling, but moved out of the way instead, initially unbeknownst to his boss and to fellow co-workers. In order to ease the workplace taunting, Jim suggests Michael make jokes about himself and the situation in front of his subordinates. Michael agrees and starts to joke about how funny it was that he fell into a koi pond at a business meeting. The employees chuckle and then start to sympathize, saying, "It could've happened to anyone, Michael," and similar sentiments. Michael takes it too far and continues to exaggerate his buffoonery, saying statements like, "I've actually been there before," which worsens the circumstance. The mood turns uncomfortable, and the topic is avoided for some time. Later that day, the office finds out Jim let Michael fall in the water by leaning away from him as Michael frantically grabbed for help. Soon enough, people in the office start leaning away from him whenever he walks past them. It's season 6, episode 8, in case you wanted to take a gander at the full thing.

    This is a great scenario because it highlights the relevance of making fun of friends; if they fall into a koi pond during a business meeting, you probably can and should give them a hard time once they cool off from their rough day. Also, if that happens to someone you know, please reach out to me and send pictures if you're able. Jim also gives Michael the proper advice when he suggests he make fun of himself to release some of the pressure. And of course, another lesson is learned as Michael continues to speak poorly of his decision-making; he quickly goes from taking the shovel from others' hands to digging his own grave. Like I said, anything in excess is too much. And finally, by the closing of the show, we see how quickly humor can be maneuvered toward or against someone. It's also just a funny episode, in my opinion. If you have a moment, treat yourself by watching "Michael Scott Koi Pond full video," which highlights the full clip of Steve Carell, the actor who plays Michael, pretending to struggle in a two-foot-deep pond. Most actors would probably make the scene feel uncomfortable or scripted, but Steve pulls it off so well.

    Additionally, this goes without saying, but this is a show. Situations don't play out as harmlessly or fluidly as they do on television, so as always, be aware and conscientious. I'm just trying to include adequate buffers to ensure nobody comes after me if someone uses my advice out of context and humor is used inappropriately. You can't say I didn't warn you. And speaking of context, be aware of audience and delivery. I think we'd all agree that making morbid jokes at a funeral is typically frowned upon, as addressed earlier. However, I'm not one to ban humor from any one situation, so wield it how you will, but doing a quick risk-to-reward analysis wouldn't be a bad idea. Let it be said, I have accidentally laughed during a funeral before, completely unintentionally, so I'm not above anybody. Well, except maybe the person we buried that day.

Something else to note about exercising caution with humor is in regard to social media platforms—be slow to post controversial things on social media or other public sites. Social scrutiny can have more of an effect than awkwardness at holiday dinners. It can impact current or potential job opportunities, education admissions, and more. I remember at my old high school there was a local outrage because some students pulled a senior prank that got them banned from walking at graduation. A classmate thought it was an opportune moment to joke on Twitter about bringing a dangerous weapon to school in retribution for his friends' punishments. Days later, he was arrested for his threat, which was intended to be taken as a light-hearted slight to the high school's administration. This otherwise smart, competent student was bound for a scholarship at a local university, but he was stripped of that opportunity following the arrest.

You are not invincible under the guise of comedy. You can't get away with threats, no matter how obvious or well-meaning. It's essential to consider the joke from an alternative perspective and acknowledge how it might appear and affect someone else. There is a not-so-fine line between a great joke and a sexual harassment charge. If you feel it might be inappropriate, especially in a professional setting, it probably isn't worth sharing. I promise I'm almost done with the "what not to do" rant, but if you're going to experiment with humor, it's necessary to throw in qualifiers.

This next one is a particular pet peeve of mine. For the love of God, do not use humor as a means for passive-aggressiveness. Contrary to popular belief, pettiness is not cool, and I won't encourage that type of humor. Pettiness is considered to be a form of passive aggression and is done as a response to someone doing something that you find displeasing. I've seen "influencers" boast their pettiness through a variety of platforms, suggesting it's a necessary evil, if claiming it as a negative at all. It drives me absolutely bonkers. Wielding humor in defense of your own immaturity is not what I'd consider a useful use of your budding abilities. It might be appropriate to use comedy as an escape or point of relief for yourself or others, but if you're the type of person who laughs at someone else while they're angry because you don't know what else to do, you're trying to buffer the awkwardness or it's a self-preservation tactic; then that would be under the "inappropriate" category.

Last, but certainly not least, pandering. Don't do it. Pandering is a means to appeal to a certain audience, but done in a distasteful, unethical, or cringey manner. Politics, for example, is drenched with those who pander; in fact, it's their chosen profession. Politicians are expected to represent the people and sometimes that's translated into doing whatever it takes to make them appear more relatable. If a Senator is called racist on live television, a week later you might find their campaign manager pushing images of the representative shaking hands and spending time with minority populations. Pandering isn't just perfected by those who hold an office, it can also include those who uncomfortably spout jokes that cater to their audience, no matter who they might be. A nicer way of labelling them could be "chameleons" because of how they change depending on whoever is present. Bo Burnham does a clever parody about how some country music styles pander. It's called *Country Song*, which can be found on YouTube. His style of humor can be dark and explicit, so keep that in mind if you decide to look for it.

Well, I suppose that's pretty much the bulk of what not to do with humor. I can't stop you from doing these things, of course, I just discourage them. I'm not too self-important to acknowledge that most of my advice is centered around my experiences and pet peeves, but I'd like to believe there's a righteous frustration to justify my opinions. But I admit, I have misled you, as there is one last "definitely don't do this" I have to offer. Humor is a finicky thing, there's no perfect formula so you can be funny all the time. There will be too many days your jokes won't land and you're the only one laughing. I don't know how many times I can reasonably reiterate this without exasperation ensuing, but that's absolutely normal. My "don't" suggestion is that you don't let it fester. Still thinking about that awkward joke that didn't land? Stop it. It was cringy and uncomfortable, but it's over. Allowing the memory to reside in your mind rent-free is damaging to your self-confidence and willingness to tell jokes, which I'm sure you've worked hard to build.

I remember one time I noticed my friend waiting to laugh until others did first, especially when he was the one telling a joke. It was one of those things where I couldn't un-notice it, but it seemed clear to me that he wasn't secure enough to make a joke and believe it was actually funny because he believed it was funny. He was one of those guys that is naturally talented at a lot of stuff, too, the kind of guy you wouldn't exactly anticipate having a hard time accepting his own self-importance. And despite his uncertainty, his jokes were funny. This is why building your confidence is so important as you improve your humor; even if you're hilarious, it doesn't matter if you don't know it or act like it.

Chapter Six: Planning Ahead

Call me a calendar because I'm a planner by nature. Before I continue, I want to acknowledge that this wasn't a good joke— I just wanted you to know I know. Carrying on: if there's a tough life decision to be made, I write a pros and cons list, if there's a vacation on the horizon there will be an itinerary, and if there's a situation to be had there's probably a joke already in the queue. Maybe I'm just Type A, but I do nearly everything I can to anticipate situations, conversations, and potential needs. If you have anxiety then you're already riding in the boat I've described, and frankly, you're probably sailing it so you can be in control. My philosophy is to be prepared now and thank yourself later. If a charger is nearby, my phone is probably plugged in, even if it doesn't need juice. At all times, my car has an extra pair of clothes, a jacket, and a container of water. I also carry chargers for both androids and iPhones, napkins, individually wrapped straws, plastic utensils, pens, ChapStick, and a small "just because" style greeting card just in case a situation arises (you'd be surprised, I've used it more than once). If you're in a relationship and always forget major dates your significant other cares about, that last one could be a lifesaver for you. I understand not everyone has a desire to be on the same caliber of preparedness, but if you're seeking out advice on increasing comfort and confidence in situations, then I suggest working on your ability to think ahead.

    We've already discussed being ready with a story or talent on hand for various social situations, so let's dive more into what it means to be prepared with a joke. One-liners and other universal-type jokes are useful to have in your back pocket, but I want to talk about planning ahead for specific situations to make it appear natural and relevant to the conversation. As a self-proclaimed professional funny person, I regularly make up jokes in anticipation for events. For example, you know you're going to be attending a wedding and you don't feel like the couple are a good fit because the bride is too friendly with her co-workers and the groom is a bit too controlling. Your friend group all recognizes this but decide it's not your place to speak up since you're all just acquaintances of the couple. And plus, I'd say there's about two categories of people who have the right to tell someone their spouse-to-be is a mistake: direct family and best friends. So, you're off the hook anyway. You all arrive to the doomed marriage ceremony and during the wedding, your buddy might make ball-and-chain jokes or reference Panic at the Disco's *I Write Sins Not Tragedies* and how the song is oddly applicable. I'd consider both of those low-hanging fruit, which isn't bad, but if you know the situation in advance and if you know your audience, which are your friends in this case, then thinking up a better joke ahead of time might be to your benefit.

    It should ideally be tailored according to your humor, but if I were in that spot, I think I would wait for an awkward moment between the not-so-happy couple and ironically say, "Man, I hope I love my spouse as much as they love each other," or, "Fingers crossed my wedding goes as great as this one." As we've established, I have a more sarcastic, dry sense of humor, so this type of joke is right up my alley. It might not be funny to you, but it's hard to communicate delivery here, or maybe it's just plainly not funny and that's fine too. Either way, I acknowledge that in this fictional situation, you're making fun of people who have graciously invited you to their special day, so if it's too mean, then draw that boundary and perhaps consider another joke that's more according to your comfort level and style of humor. Alternatively, if this sounds good to you then feel free to lock it away for an inevitably bad future wedding ceremony.

This reminds me of one particular joke I tucked away for my eventual marriage; this was thought up years prior to my engagement, mind you. It's not a good joke, but for some reason, I was intent on hanging on to it. I don't really want to tell you because I don't want to come across as unfunny and it's not exactly a quality example of comedy. However, I've already committed to my previous not-so-funny jokes, so if I haven't impressed you yet then I'm afraid I would be out of luck anyway. Additionally, it helps that I'm content in enjoying my own humor, so I'll just assume it's good stuff and share anyway. All weddings have something that doesn't go according to plan, that's just how complex events go. When something goes wrong or plays out in an unideal way, I planned to nonchalantly say, "Come on guys, let's get this right. I only plan to get married two or three times so I want this one to count." It's not my best work, I know, but for reasons unknown I always kept it in mind. Plus, for what's it's worth, I told it to my friend and her boyfriend because it was somehow relevant to our conversation at the time and her boyfriend couldn't stop laughing about it. I was shocked because it seemed a little underwhelming to me, but he just *got* it for reasons I can't explain. His reception is a good reminder that we can't control how people respond to our jokes, for worse or for better. It's important to take the good responses well and the let the uninspired ones roll off your back. In this case, I've remembered his bursting laughter for several years because I'm proud of that joke, even if it wasn't that great.

Always keep in mind that, just like confidence, humor is internal. It's fun to put on a show for people to enjoy as well, but you should use humor for your own enjoyment; this will also feed into feeling confident in yourself. An added perk of finding yourself hilarious is that the people who love you will enjoy you telling the joke, even if they don't enjoy the actual joke. Remember when I said find a humor style that comes naturally to you? Well, get ready to groan because I identify with puns. This may be well established, as you've presumably read a lot of examples of this type of humor prior to this section, but it'll still surprise you. We've already gone through the socially acceptable response when someone executes a pun, but just a reminder: you'll want to scrunch up your face, tilt it to the side, and do some sort of disapproving sigh in protest of the inevitably bad joke you were just told. A light, pitiful laugh is also acceptable if it was particularly bad (good) or unexpected. This is just how it's done, I'm just here to socialize you in case you need a refresher on how to be a human in this cut-throat, comedy-driven society. While people appreciating you is not the goal of humor, it's always nice to feel secure even in the midst of your most absurdly unfunny pun. I believe old proverbs have detailed the following riddle: "What is better the worse it is?" Congratulations, even garbage puns are quality jokes according to this saying I just exaggerated.

Sometimes you'll pull a muscle trying to stretch out your joke to apply to a certain situation; I've hurt myself many-a-times overextending a pun or two. Which reminds me, there's this joke I can't seem to put together and it's driving me bonkers. It's a pun and, like many good puns, it takes a bit of mental gymnastics. I'm trying to connect injustice to in-jest-us, but I can't seem to get it right. The premise is something about a marginalized group debating a heavy topic, so it might be appropriate to consider in-jest-us (injustice) for some comic relief…or something. Like I said, I really can't get it. If someone out there finishes this poetic joke, please let me know, and also thank you. I'm not exactly sure how I can apply the injustice/in-jest-us joke in the wild, but that's the challenging parts of Pun Olympics I love. Maybe if I complete this scenario where it actually makes sense I'll figure it out. However, I don't exclusively plan puns or jokes in advance, I do live performances in the wild, too.

I've already got a joke in queue intended to be used after this piece is published. When a conversation about humor or confidence comes up down the road, I'll contribute to the conversation and then say, "It's not like I wrote the book on confidence/humor—oh wait, I guess I kind of did!" I doesn't matter whether you find that funny because I do. I enjoy both sides of humor that's aimed at the self, whether intended to blithely, ironically gasconade or to poke fun at myself. As I've mentioned a few times, self-deprecating humor is the bee's knees these days, so right after we're done instilling confidence, you'll have to start applying your newly learned humor to knock it right back down. So get ready and good luck.

Planning ahead can help you feel more confident with your joke, take some of the stress out of the delivery, and help you execute a great line seemingly on the spot. Up to this point we've talked about how execution might work according to the audience, but we're going to go into further detail about what that might actually look like. As you've been told and re-told as an artist, writer, performer, or just plain human being, be aware of your audience and adjust accordingly; it's in their best interest and yours. The jokes I tell around my devoutly religious parents, for example, are not the same jokes I tell friends, and vice versa. I'm hoping this doesn't need to be answered, but you might be asking why this is the case, so I'll address it anyway. In this situation, it's because my friends' styles of humor are more aligned with my own, and even if they weren't, they're more aware of current humor trends. I've already told you of my dad's misinterpretation of a satirical article I wrote using humor as a mask for modern day self-deprecation. I know I can't tell a lot of the same jokes around my parents and their friends as I would around my own friends, and that's okay. This is especially true when you consider my styles of humor revolve around more dark, dry humor than the next person. Puns, however, reign free in my parent's household and that is fair game. My mom isn't a huge fan, but my dad awards me a little chuckle, and that's enough.

This doesn't mean that you can't play with your audience to gauge their level of enthusiasm and connection with a specific type of humor. In fact, I encourage the trial-and-error process. Let the record show that I suggest you be more modest than aggressive as you get a feel for your audience, going slower and building up, but I'd be lying if I said it's the approach I always take. I'm sure you've picked it up, but I prefer to commit to my jokes first and then bear the positive or negative consequences afterward. It's high risk, high reward. I've no doubt had to deal with discomfort because of this method, but I've also gotten job offers because of it. I primarily let professionalism drive during job interviews, so I'm not spewing jokes every other minute, but I try to let my guard down a bit to show I've got some personality underneath my qualifications. Although employers appreciate professionalism, they also want to know who they're hiring and what to expect if they do hire you.

Even though I insist you take your audience into account, I want to revisit something I discouraged in the previous chapter. Appealing to your audience is good, but pandering is not. At this point, it's important to categorize my view of pandering; this isn't something I see as a thing that could be neutral, although some people that qualify would consider it to be harmless. To me, pandering is excessive, unnecessary, and tactless. If you define it differently, then this point of discouragement isn't necessarily meant for you; but if you pander in the same way "nice guys" do, then you're probably going to have a bad time and then wonder why it's not working. In this context, "nice guys" are referred to as guys who pretend to be friendly, polite, or complimentary but turn on you the moment their target expresses any form of lack of interest; it should be noted that "nice girls" absolutely exist as well. To use in a sentence: nice guys pander to girls so they seem like a pleasant person, but only use their forced charm for their own interests.

Another footnote that I'll reiterate until I'm blue in the face is that humor, again, should be primarily for your enjoyment. The audience helps you gauge what direction to go with humor and, like I've mentioned, it feels good to be reinforced by a positive reaction, but their reaction is not your responsibility. Use it to have a good time. I make jokes to myself, for myself, all of the time. Sometimes I'll realize they're actually really good and I remember them for another, more public occasion, and sometimes they're so bad I keep it to myself. There are some moments where I'll recount how ridiculous my joke was to a close friend, kind of poking fun at my dorky style of humor and the fact that I do it when I'm alone. In a way, this is also a form of a joke, sort of a joke inception—a joke within a joke. If I'm making fun of myself and a previous awful joke, this retelling constitutes as humor as well, especially because we're probably both laughing at my past self.

In order to plan jokes ahead of time, it might be useful to consider the overlap you share with the people who will probably be at your joke's debut. There are tons of overlap the average American relates with and countless jokes are funny because of that similarity. One time I heard someone say that November, Thursday, and the color purple all pretty much give off the same impression. I have no idea what it means, and I can't explain it, but that just makes sense to me, and it did for a lot of other people. How can so many other people take nonsense information and agree sense out of it? It's because of some weird overlap that we can't identify. Occasionally you'll see a person who has a name you did not expect.

The common fad going around is to call suburban, white moms "Karen." Personally, I'm of the opinion that it's overused and an extreme generalization, but there's a reason it's become such an infamous trend. Karen is a very popular name for the stereotyped demographic and enough people have associated a specific attitude, attire, and appearance that everyone has an image in their head of who a "Karen" is if referred to in a story. There's also a reason jokes about Mondays, tax season, corporate America, politics, and religion can land so well—almost everyone can relate with the frustration of most of those things.

The insurance company Geico takes a lot of these familiar ideas and runs with it. They take common tropes, such as a monotonous businessman, caveman, animated pig, and rhetorical questions to illustrate their company's famous motto, "Geico can save you 15% or more on car insurance."

It's one of those quotes you already know because of how often you hear it. Their "It's What You Do" special includes social norms that we tend to adhere to, and they'll usually add a twist. One of my personal favorites is "If you're a golf commentator, you whisper," and the camera reveals golf commentators speaking softly despite a Kraken erupting from the water. This example takes real-life experience and expectations and brings a fun, unexpected factor. I admit I'm a corporate pawn, but I love these commercials. Their marketing department needs a raise. By coincidence or not, I do have Geico insurance, so there you go, the power of comedy.

If you're not sure where else to start to plan ahead, write out a list of relatable things. What do we, as human beings, all deal with? It could be sleep deprivation, poor mental health, paper cuts, your belt loop hooking on a door, stubbing your toe, bad connection, dreading exercise, appeasing your boss, or dealing with telemarketers. I recognize these are all bad, but it's far easier to laugh at the unfortunate things that happen than the good things for some reason.

There are millions of small things that we have to go through that are relatable. Close the gap and look for a funny twist, an appropriate context, and a stellar way to deliver it. People like associating with content, which is part of the reason I've used so many references from other TV shows, movies, and books. We're also suckers for nostalgia, so making a joke around a reference from the '90s will give you an easier time landing it, with the right audience. But this is why we plan ahead, right?

PART III: APPLYING BOTH

CHAPTER SEVEN: THE PURPOSE

You might be thinking, "This is all ridiculous; why do we even need confidence?" or "Why do we care about humor anyway?" We know self-confidence and funniness are important traits to tote around and can be useful in scoring a date or job opportunity, but logically, you might not be able to explain what about them makes others so much more likeable. I'd like to delve into an explanation for why they hold value to ourselves and to society. To some, this may be the boring part, and to others this may be the most intriguing, but either way I feel I'm obligated to insist you stick around because I think it's valuable stuff, but I admit I'm biased; I'm in the camp of being intrigued by this type of thing. I'm going to outline a bit about humor and confidence, starting with the former.

In my research, I've noticed humor is like intelligence: it's ambiguous, hard to define, and is presented in different ways depending on the culture or person. There are somewhat universal ways to determine humor or intelligence, but there's nothing psychologically set to definitely pinpoint what makes someone funny or smart. If you're a people-pleaser, you may feel the need to find that switch in your brain to deliver better jokes; in this case, it might feel like a mode of survival. Charles Darwin predicted humor is for social play and building rapport and Sigmund Freud believed its intention was to release tension. Perhaps those names are familiar, and you don't know why, so lest you can't think of it, here's a reminder: Charles Darwin is infamous for his study of evolution, particularly his research on the Galapagos Islands, in which he observed a variety of animals' evolutionary patterns, which had adapted to survive to different conditions. His background is relevant to this topic because his bread and butter is exploring natural selection and survival. His interest in the subject alone communicates the importance of humor. Sigmund Freud is referred to as the father of psychology and is said to be the first recorded psychoanalyst. His history is necessary to consider because he made great strides in the field of psychology and worked to explain human behavior and cognition, setting misogyny and insanity aside.

A version of philosopher Immanuel Kant's theory is arguably the most accepted explanation for humor's prevalence, which is highlighted in his book *Critique of Pure Reason*: "Laughter is an affection arising from the sudden transformation of a strained expectation into nothing." Of course, there are circumstances where you are expecting something funny and are amused nonetheless, such as stand-up comedy, meme pages, and reading this book. But of course, we know that, like intelligence, humor isn't universally understood and accepted in the same ways. There are a variety of considerations when discussing applicable humor, two of which involve culture and time period. We've reviewed that Eastern and Western cultures primarily utilize humor for different purposes, one intended to communicate a point and the other to relieve stress, the latter of which Freud suggests.

At this point, you might be wondering why self-deprecating humor exists, since it seems relevant to this time period. I'm sure others more qualified than I have better theories, but I think it's at least partly because of the natural shifts in society. Have you ever heard of the cultural Me versus We pendulum swing? The theory is that society's public opinion changes between me-focused to we-focused every 40 years or so. In between those 40 years, it's gradually leaning toward one side, so it's very rarely 100% Me or 100% We, it typically trends toward one side or the other until it reaches its peak, and then promptly swings back. According to the theory, we started to emerge out of the "Me" stance in 2003, which started around 1963, and have begun transitioning into "We" since that point, which is proposed to continue until 2043. As the pendulum swings back to the We side, psychologists suggest we're shifting our attention to more social justice movements that impact the masses rather than the individual. There are pros and cons to each one. We, for example, encourages conformity and unity, which can quickly turn into negative traits. Me, on the other hand, prioritizes more significant change rather than little steps, but it is driven by self-interest and personal liberty. You may have a preference for how society operates, but hopefully you can see the benefits and shortcomings of each. But back to my own hypothesis; I think cycling to the We side makes it easier for us to discredit us, as the individuals.

I read some stranger's social media post which voiced a concern for how they could foresee our society already starting to make our way to the other side. Their point was not driven on the basis that especially significant signs of self-importance are being presented in our current thinking, but on the basis that there's a massive mental health movement. The stranger's concern arises from an over-emphasis on self-care, which could potentially drive us to exclusively worry about taking care of our own needs rather than our neighbors'. You can disagree with this thought process, or the pendulum theory as a whole, but this all serves as a possible reason as to why certain types of humor come and go in trends. Very few of us have lived lives complete enough to experience full cycles of both We and Me, so it's difficult to say whether there's been an actual notice of the nuanced shifts of humor across, say, 80 years.

It should also be noted that this varies across cultures; I'm unsure if this theory would apply to other countries as well, but this is mainly based on the trends of the United States. Western cultures are predominantly individualistic, which means its residents focus on the self; whereas Eastern cultures tend to be collectivist, which considers the people as a whole more than the self. This begs the question: does the pendulum swing theory relate to other cultures as well? If so, how does the "We" apply to individualistic cultures versus collectivist, and how does the "Me" apply to collectivist cultures versus individualist? The connotation of the theory is that we're toggling between these two types of cultural focuses, but how does that apply to the overall society's core values? Food for thought or topics to research, depending on your preference. This theory applying to self-deprecating humor specifically is not a hill I'll die on, but I absolutely think this type of societal shift has an impact on personal habits and nationwide trends.

In her book, *The Cognitive Neuroscience of Humor*, Sheila M. Kennison agrees with early Charles Darwin theories involving the advantage humor provides for rapport-building and social play. In addition to those benefits, humor can also be a great tool in diffusing conflicts, which points to its success in the natural selection process. Similarly, Kennison hypothesizes that humor is a useful trait from a biological perspective because it can spare someone from harm or even death; therefore, it's in the species' best interest to continue these genes through selective reproduction. Additionally, research reinforces the theory that intelligence and humor are positively correlated due to humor's activation of several different parts of the brain, such as language, cognition, and gratification.

This is a great perspective because we oftentimes consider the positive impact humor grants on a social level, but it's easy to neglect the biological purpose of humor. The human body and brain might seem haphazardly put together in some respects (such as the presence of vestigial body parts, like a tailbone) and meticulously orchestrated in others, but it looks like the presence of playfulness and whimsy are not accidental. A journal article by David Rousell suggests the importance of humor in our lives creates a physical wave-like presence as we laugh; he describes it as "felt vitality that strikes the body directly." Scientists and researchers continue to study humor and its part in our lives and biology. We're still learning about it, especially how it impacts the brain, but there seems to be a consensus that it's more important than simply gaining charisma points.

I've mentioned in passing that humor is a great point of attraction as well. I suggested that this type of gene is reproductively ideal in view of survival, but it's also an ideal trait we recognize at the front of our consciousness, too. Many people picture their ideal partner to be funny or have the same type of humor. Fact is, funny people are just a good time. It helps to be outgoing and funny, that's the dream combo, but sometimes it just doesn't work out that way. I'm sure we all know that one person who says one word for everybody else's five hundredth word, but every time they open their mouth it's either hilarious or profound. Well, I'm assuming everyone knows someone like that. If you don't, it's a sight to behold; they seem to pipe in when you least expect it. Maybe it's best to throw out this whole book and listen to those types of people: shut up, pay attention, and formulate your responses carefully. I can't speak for you, but I'd never be able to pull that off. If you can relate, do that; if you can't, don't do that. Simple enough. Another helpful tip from yours truly. I know what you're thinking, this must be the 1850s because you've hit the gold rush. Keep panning for treasure, my friend, because these gold nuggets of wisdom will continue to flow.

The more it's revealed, the more it just makes sense that we have something like humor. The more developed our world gets the more difficult it is to enjoy life, which is ironic because we're immersing deeper into a world of convenience as time goes on. I think about Pixar's *Wall-E* far too often. If you haven't seen it, the premise is that humans have overused Earth to the point of utter depletion of life; from what we could tell, there were no animals or vegetation. Humans couldn't live that way, so a major cooperation flew them into space on massive ships that were effectively space cruises. Robots regularly left the cruise ships to do an evaluation of our old planet to see if life had returned; if proof of vegetation were to be provided by these robots, the humans would return and colonize again. In the meantime, we see what mankind has become. Centuries of living in these space cruisers go by and humans have become completely sedentary due to levitating chairs, food and drink on demand, screens attached to their chairs, and other conveniences. They move around the ship in their little vehicles, chatting through screens and watching material, and that is their whole existence.

I think about it so frequently because in a way, isn't that what we're working toward? Granted, we're not conquering technological feats so we can stay stationary from birth to death, but in the age of convenience and growth, we're certainly heading in that direction. It can be so difficult to enjoy life sometimes because it feels like we're checking off boxes to get through it. Is it just me? Go to work and get paid. Check. Hang out with friends this month. Check. Get married and have kids. Check. And then what, you know? This is all more existential than you possibly have signed up for, but these are considerations when we're looking at the purpose for humor. All those little checkpoints we make through our life are spaced out by relationships and laughter. I know I'm not the only one who feels like a corporate drudge sometimes, even though I'm so thankful for a consistent job. It's hard not to go back and forth between gratefulness at a comfortable life and the frustrations the day-to-day brings, but comedy breaks it all up. It's the most socially acceptable and accessible form of a tension release. Convenience is becoming the expectation, but humor is ever-changing and because it adapts with the times, it feels new and never outdated.

You could say the value of confidence also does not have an expiration date. There's a need for confidence, just like for humor, whether it be for survival, social sanity, or pleasure. But why be confident in the first place? People go their whole lives without feeling secure in who they are, and they've made it through, right? Well, I think you already see the value in maintaining confidence because you're reading this, but I'll get into it anyway. After all, it's always nice to be able to affirm what you know to be true. Like what we talked about before, we know certain people have advantages; it could be due to attractiveness, race, personality, social status, wealth, and so forth. It undeniably exists, even if we can't quite put our finger on some of the reasons.

Research suggests that confident people are more open to new experiences, and this includes opportunities that would have otherwise been missed. It's also cyclical, which means you can improve motivation to continue building self-confidence if you've already got a good foundation. It's like working out—the first three months are the absolute hardest. Even on the days you feel good, it's still hard to do it over and over again. But as you continue to exercise according to a regular routine, working out starts to feel more beneficial than the energy you exert into it. Unless you run. If you're a runner then bless your heart, I imagine you're just always in pain all the time. Similarly, as the motivation increases, so does your resilience, for both self-confidence and working out. Joyce Brothers, a psychologist, says, "Women who are confident of their abilities are more likely to succeed than those who lack confidence, even though the latter may be much more competent and talented and industrious." She primarily worked with women, but this applies to men too.

Gaining confidence affords you a comfort convenience cannot. You'll start to feel comfortable in circumstances that would probably have made you anxious. Even in new, unfamiliar situations, you won't constantly be assuming whether you're doing something wrong, if you're at the right place, if you've read the instructions correctly, and so forth. Again, I'll be careful not to present this like an ego trip, because it's different. I'm not trying to add cockiness to your life; I'm hoping to take away the discomforts that uncertainty brings. Remember that ego is driven from a place of self-preservation and self-promotion, whereas confidence is driven by your belief in yourself. This is how I've come to the conclusion that humility and confidence play into each other, while ego and low self-esteem feed into each other. Ambition is awesome, and I want to make this distinction now, but spilling paint on others just to make yourself shine is not the same thing. By the way, I just made up the metaphor, so feel free to get that cycling through everyday language. I'd love to hear that pop up in surprising ways, so thank you for your efforts.

I get that it can feel similar between ego and confidence. Maybe you've already got it down by now, but because I like to solidify my points, let's play another game. I don't have a fancy name for this one, so let's just call it "Confidence or Cockiness." Just like before, I'll offer some scenarios and you'll assign one or the other to each one.

First one: A co-worker is critiquing Dom's work and Dom responds back, "I'm the most competent person in the department with Excel; I'm doing this right."

Number two: You've held the number one ranking for Super Mario Bros on your family's old Nintendo Console for decades. Recently you were re-hashing old memories with your siblings and you all decided to play it again. Weeks later, your sibling finally beat your high score, so you say, "Yeah, for now. Give me a day, I'll get my place back."

And I have a third: it's Friday and most of the floor works half days on Fridays. James and several others are remaining, but there's still plenty of work to be done. A colleague comes up to him and says they need to split up extra work to compensate for an entry-level worker's missing documents. James refuses because he knows that he wasn't hired for this role, it's not his responsibility, and it's below his skill level.

Okay, so which do you think applies where? I'd say scenario one is confidence, but this comes with a need for situational awareness. If this is day one of the new job and someone is trying to guide Dom according to their policies, and Dom retorts by claiming they're certainly the best person in the department, that can easily be driven by ego. However, if they're a senior manager and it has been proven by their work and position that they know exactly what they're doing, I'd consider standing up for Dom's workplace competence is absolute confidence. I know this can get tricky in professional environments. I know a lot of people, particularly the younger generation and more often women, are more inclined to add what I call fluff to business emails. This fluff would include many pleasantries, excessive exclamation marks, profuse apologies, and a meekness toward pointing out another's mistake; the last one is more problematic than fluff, but you get the gist.

And what do you think of number two—Confidence or Cockiness? This one I'd attribute to cockiness because while you've proven you are proficient at the game, assuming you'll beat your sibling in this case is more of a cocky move. Again, this is all taken with a grain of salt and the answer may vary with the situation. If playful, then confidence and cockiness may not come into the picture at all; it could be a harmless competition between siblings.

Thirdly, I've left this one intentionally open to interpretation. This person may sound rude or like he's not a team player for picking up lower level's slack, but it also isn't his job to do other people's work, especially if the others just didn't do it. But on the other hand, if James refuses because he sees the work as beneath him, then that could be an issue. A good trick to see if ego is getting in the way or not is to determine if any work is beneath you, or the person in question. All good leaders are willing to roll up their sleeves and put in the work on the ground.

I worked as a server through college and my boss was always really tough. If anyone made a mistake or if it was busy and he was just stressed, he'd communicate his frustrations to the rest of the staff. I can't tell you how often that guy made me mad while I was just trying to do my job. But, when things got busy, he filled whatever gap he could. If we needed someone to host, run food, get ice, cook, appease customers, whatever it was, he stepped up, and it was evident that nothing was beneath him. Despite his brash management style, I've always respected that about him, and I think every good leader, manager, and boss has that quality. Great leaders have confidence, not ego.

Back in Part I, I mentioned learned helplessness, which can be caused by having an external locus of control. A quick refresher: the external locus of control states that you place responsibility in external factors, such as environmental causes that are outside your control. Learned helplessness suggests that thoughts or feelings of powerlessness are reinforced by a learned fear of failure. I'll provide an illustration to better describe learned helplessness. I'm not sure if the practice of this is actually true, but it is said that in circuses or zoos, baby elephants would be tied up with a basic rope around their leg. At their age and size, they don't have the strength to break the rope and escape, which they discover quickly. Because they've tried and tried to break this rope in the past, they know it's not something they're able to do. However, they maintain this belief into adulthood, so supposedly, that measly rope will contain an adult elephant because it assumes itself to be trapped, just like they were as a tiny elephant. Poor guys. This isn't relevant to the actual example, but from a social perspective, I wonder if a new, grown elephant were to be introduced to that circus or zoo, would that elephant learn helplessness as well, but instead of learning through their own experience, would they learn through socialization? Just a thought.

Hopefully, that example was useful in describing learned helplessness; it's essentially a form of conditioning. Clinicians theorize it could be an underlying cause of depression, which is interesting when considering the positive correlation between self-esteem and depression. This is an important thing to address because a lot of irrational thoughts come from this concept. I'm doing a lot of call-backs, so get ready to flip back and forth if needed. Cognitive Behavioral Therapy (CBT), you may remember, deals with irrational thoughts. The purpose of this type of therapy is to recognize these types of thoughts, correct them, and your behavior should follow. Try to think of a situation in your life where you assume you'll fail because of past experiences. A drug addict has tried to get clean for years and has been met with no long-term success, so their assumption that they can't succeed is learned. Someone struggling with anxiety might stop themselves from going on a badly needed trip to the store because last time they had a panic attack.

Professionals suggest learned helplessness is a response to a previous trauma and the individual doesn't believe it was confined to the one scenario and they believe that it cannot be controlled. One of the most difficult things about beating this phenomenon is the baby steps it requires to work your way out of it. Can't quit smoking because you've tried and failed? Cut your intake in half, or if that's too much, cut it by a third. Any progress is progress. CBT is also a great tool to combat learned helplessness, which can be applied during counseling sessions and to use as a reference point for growth as well. You don't need to be a professional to identify corruptive thoughts and redirect them to positive, productive thoughts. You should also know that there's such thing as learned optimism as well, which is nurtured by being kind to yourself and promoting a positive internal voice. Just like the effects of learned helplessness, learned optimism can work in your benefit.

You know, I first decided to go into the psychology and mental health field because of the impact confidence has on people. Insecurity is devastating and can reduce quality of life so significantly that someone would rather not live just to take the pain of inadequacy away. I'm not saying people who aren't confident must surely be suicidal or depressed, that's a broad generalization that I don't agree with, but it's undeniable that insecurity is a factor in mental wellness and the will to live. Confidence isn't just charisma or an ideal quality to look for in a partner—it's a cornerstone of life. You may identify with the crippling feeling of insignificance or maybe you've never experienced that, but either way, confidence leaks and spills and potentially wreaks havoc on almost every part of your life. I've said this before and I'll keep saying it: having self-confidence is not a privilege of being human, it's a right. It's a moral obligation to respect what you've got, even if what you've got isn't that great in your eyes.

If you struggle with finding meaning in your life and feel like you lack confidence because of it, Viktor Frankl's *Man's Search for Meaning* is a humbling, breath-taking read that I will recommend every chance I get. I've known it to change perspectives and lives. I know I've dumped a lot of recommendations on you. I'd obviously encourage exploration of all of them, but I'm doing my best to equip you with as many resources as possible. I'd rather you get through some of them than give up because there's too many, and that's assuming you've been making a note of every single thing I've suggested, which, let's be real, is incredibly unlikely. Read, watch, and absorb what you can and, as always, give yourself some grace for what you can't. I think these resources can be helpful for you and I hope you go as slowly or quickly as you need. The famous quote that's attributed to Confucius goes, "It doesn't matter how slow you go as long as you don't stop."

Keep moving, keep fighting, and keep working toward a better you. You're great as you are now, but there's someone more matured and self-assured waiting for you tomorrow.

Chapter Eight: Awareness

Before jumping into the meat of this chapter, I want to appreciate how far you've come to reach this point. Acknowledging constructive steps that you've chosen to take is so important because we tend to be harsher on ourselves, forgetting the good things we've done and capitalizing on the bad, to the point of remembering or punishing ourselves years after the fact. You've got to take the time to enjoy the progress you've made, even if it feels like you haven't done anything tangible yet. Just by reading this, you've taken a practical, forward step. And if by the end you still feel stuck, go back to some of the sections where I offer specific advice on comedians to watch, confidence tricks to pull, and the like. Rereading things you've already read can be helpful because minute by minute we change, in our perception, mood, motivation, and reception. This book will not help you solve your issues, this isn't some guidebook you can rely on like a safety crutch providing universal answers, but I challenge you to commit to these approaches, they're here for a reason. Keep on reading, because this is not the point in which my infallible concrete suggestions have expired—more will come in a few paragraphs. But for now, I insist you take a metaphorical step back and pat yourself on the back for wanting to be better and for taking active steps to get there. After you've done that, we can revisit the power of awareness and how it can affect you.

  Building confidence and humor mean almost nothing if there's no effort or awareness to recognize the improvement along the way. The reason it means nothing is because it's almost impossible to continue growing if you don't acknowledge that growth. What if companies operated without comparing themselves to the previous month or year, or without considering the strides and successes of their competitors? Executive officers would stand up in the big quarterly meeting and say things like, "I don't *feel* like we've made a big impact. To me, our numbers seem the same this September as it did September of last year." And of course, they'll inevitably work to amend this lack of change they haven't sensed: "Okay, it looks like we've got to start from scratch and rebuild our strategy" or possibly "Okay, it looks like this division isn't doing its job since it seems like performance has either regressed or stayed the same, we'll have to let them go." I don't need to point out this doesn't make any sense. How often do we feel like we've made no progress on something just because it's moving slowly? Even if we track the development and agree it's improving slowly, it's hard not to forget how far we've come, and there's a need to go back and remind yourself that things are doing better. Anyone who's been in therapy can attest to the fact that growth is not linear, and it is so maddeningly gradual it feels like no progress is being made whatsoever.

    The human spirit tends to be incredibly sensitive, and I say this as a human, so this applies to me too. I always check those Captcha "I'm not a robot" boxes, so I don't know what more proof you need. As non-robots, it's easy for us to get discouraged if we don't feel satisfaction, praise, or growth in the process of something difficult. This affirmation doesn't even need to be from others, sometimes it's something we can and should be granting ourselves. It can be frustrating being programmed this way, but it's how most of us are built. Requiring confirmation to upkeep motivation is natural. Self-improvement must entail acknowledging the progress along the way; you don't need to record the frequency, length, and strength of your friend's laughter over time in order to figure out if you've gotten funnier, but you probably do need something to help you recognize how far you've come. Despite your initial instinct to avoid something like this, it's not a bad idea to ask around to get an idea of where other people think you're at. It may feel lame or awkward but asking friends you trust if you've gotten funnier is a good benchmark to see if other people think you've gotten better. You can only be aware of so much, after all. The same goes for confidence. Hopefully, you know people you can confide in to ask this possibly uncomfortable question, but it's the only real way to get a slightly impartial, third-party take on the potential changes to your behavior. Maybe you've gotten insufferable, and you just don't know it, but that's what friends are for.

It might be hard for people to gauge if and how you've grown to be more confident and funnier, so it would also be useful to lay down seeds ahead of time. Ask them to try to observe your behavior and have them notice your efforts to grow in the ways you want to better yourself. You can also use this request as an opportunity for accountability, just like we discussed with certain websites like Stickk. This site can also be used for accountability on the specific things I've suggested. Push yourself to watch ten videos a week, or more, to expose yourself to more comedy. Set aside two hours a week to people watch and take note of people who make others laugh and people who appear confident. I'll elaborate on this later, but the accountability Stickk provides can also be used for staying consistent with a journal, behavior log, or daily list of positive things that happened in a day. There's plenty described in this book that would be beneficial for you to be committed to, especially with a buddy making sure you're staying on top of it.

Gaining outside input is incredibly valuable, but it isn't the only way to track your progress. So how else do we combat our natural tendency to assume the negative? My personal favorite way is what's called a pretest-posttest design, which is used by researchers to compare the participants' knowledge or awareness about a topic before the experiment is conducted to after. For example, this is a perfect tool for discovering the efficacy of new curriculum options. If comparing two new educational modules, there would likely be three groups: one being taught Curriculum A, one being taught Curriculum B, and one not being taught anything additional so they can pose as a control group. If the researchers are feeling crazy, they can throw in a fourth group that's using a placebo by feeding them information irrelevant to the actual topic or by using the previous curriculum. Each group will take a pretest before the dependent variable, the curriculum, is introduced. After the experiment is completed and the new material is taught, each group will take a posttest, which is the same exact assessment as the pretest. After data analysis, the researchers can identify how each respective group has grown, which is the most effective, and which aspects of the curriculum need improvement. This is the same concept that brought you standardized tests at the elementary, middle, and high school levels. I'm not responsible for these borderline offensive tests, but I do apologize if you had to undergo these types of stress-inducing assessments for the sake of the following year's curriculum. You're what they call guinea pigs.

I'm not insinuating you need to find an actual test to evaluate your confidence or humor and continually take these tests until you're where you want to be. It may not be reasonable to find and complete a standardized exam testing your level of self-confidence and humor, and I'm doubtful reliable tests like that exist, but there are other ways to compare direct growth. If you do find one though, that would be convenient. Until that time comes, or unless you're uninterested in the prospect of putting yourself to the test, I suggest creating an Excel document to record information about each day. I did this for a while and, if nothing else, it was interesting to see the changes of my mood according to the things going on in my life. For example, if I wasn't performing according to my expectations at work, my mood tended to be negative throughout the week and it decreased my job and life satisfaction. There were several categories I included to this behavior log, such as total steps for the day, a general gist of what I did throughout the day, my exercise routine if applicable, whether I stretched, and overall mood, which I represented by filling the cell green, yellow, or red for a good, neutral, or bad day, respectively. I would also encourage you to include three good things that happened throughout the day, as to hold yourself accountable.

  To satisfy anyone interested, I looked back at the behavior log I completed from last year. The month from a year ago reflected how my moods varied in those thirty days. I had thirteen good (green) days, twelve neutral (yellow) days, and five bad (red) days. I looked at the notes from the month and it looks like I had exceeded my work expectations for that month, so that's what an average month of me doing well at work looks like. Interesting or not, there you have it. My work performance might impact my mood day-to-day, and it might not. A month isn't a very good sample size for something like that, which is why it's best to record consistently for at least six months, if possible.

This logging method is particularly useful for mental health because you're able to see how certain things, like your mood, are affected by external factors. Has your activity been extremely low this past week? If so, could that be why your body is lacking energy and motivation? Could the weather be directly impacting your mental health? Obviously, life isn't always as cut-and-dry as the data I'm suggesting because tons of other factors can come into play, such as social connection, productivity, work performance, sleep, weight, food, and more. All of this information might be helpful to reviewing patterns to help you be successful, but it may not be realistic to undertake all of these considerations if it's going to be something you log long-term. For the sake of this book's purpose, I suggest you include some sort of rating for confidence in a day and some sort of rating for humor. Rating these things on a scale of one to ten will hopefully reveal what habits are working, holding you back, or not affecting things.

If you're not overly competent with Excel, that's okay, it's easy to set it up. I'm sure you can look up a behavior log template online, but you don't need to use someone else's preferences if those options aren't ideal. And you certainly don't need to make one that's super fancy, like some others you might run into. Open up a blank spreadsheet using Excel Documents or Google Sheets, label the first column "Date." Type in the date in however format you want, I set it up as "Day of the Week, Month Day, Year" (i.e., Wednesday, April 22, 2020). Write a few consecutive dates in the same column and once you have two or three written, highlight those cells and drag the bottom right corner down through the blank column. Keep going for however long you'd like and it should auto-predict the date sequence you've established. If my description is confusing, there are simple YouTube tutorials to explain it more thoroughly and with visual aids, but keep in mind, this is the hardest part of setting up the document. You could also manually enter the dates as you go if you're spending too long on the set-up. Once you have the dates arranged, you'll title Column B Row 1 as the first thing you want to measure, whether that be confidence/humor rating, mood, three good things, or whatnot. Repeat for the following columns until you have everything you want to record day-by-day. Here's a general example I've created to help illustrate how it might look.

Date	Confidence Rating	Humor Rating	Mood	Weather
Wednesday, April 22, 2020	6	4		Overcast
Thursday, April 23, 2020	8	7		Sunny
Friday, April 24, 2020	5	6		Sunny
Saturday, April 25, 2020	3	6		Rainy

You can probably guess I'll urge you to include something about your day, such as listing a few good things or your general agenda (i.e., "Work, hung out with Kevin, cooked, watched TV"). And if you'd like, you can get fancy with it and associate colors to the data if you're feeling really crazy. For example, let's say you're rating your confidence for each day from one to ten and you want more of a visual representation so it's easy to skim and pick out patterns. You can assign ratings 1-3 as bad by automatically filling the cell with red after entering in the figure, then 4-6 can be neutral, with the cell filling yellow, and 7-10 can fill green for good. This is an example of how the figure above would look if you added this feature, as well as a title row using the merge cell option. You'll also notice I added a border between the colors to make them appear more distinct per column.

Behavior Log

Date	Confidence Rating	Humor Rating	Mood	Weather
Wednesday, April 22, 2020	6	4		Overcast
Thursday, April 23, 2020	8	7		Sunny
Friday, April 24, 2020	5	6		Sunny
Saturday, April 25, 2020	3	6		Rainy

  I truly think building this habit can help most people, especially if you limit it to a quick, five-minute routine at the end of your day. However, if you try to overload this log with all the features I talked about and more, it can quickly turn into a 10–15-minute chore you'll dread and eventually avoid. In general, all of this may be a bit much for some of you, but as I've mentioned earlier, I'm just here to pitch ideas for you to try; see what sticks and if doesn't work for you then that's okay. As always, I challenge you to give it a shot so you can have a realistic idea if it works for you.

  Another way to track your progress is by journaling. It may seem like a big investment of time, or at least it did to me when I first considered it, but it can be as limited or extensive as you'd like. You can set a reminder in your phone to write something weekly or daily. It can include a simple sentence of how you felt, what you did, and/or what was unique about the day or week, or it can be more of a recounting or rant. These days, I mainly journal to rant, so if you were to take a look at what I've written lately, you would just think I live an angry life, which isn't totally wrong. I am a pretty angry person overall, 5'3" and ready to throw hands. Also, keep in mind journaling doesn't have to happen in some cutesy notebook; I use a simple Word document to keep track of mine. And no, this book is not sponsored by Microsoft Office, it's not my fault their applications are everywhere.

Journaling can be an alternant or addition to the mood spreadsheet we just reviewed. You can take the pointers I've offered, but this is your record, and you can alter it to how you see fit. In fact, it's imperative you do change it according to how it works for you, because it is more likely you'll be able to follow through with it if you're following your own guidelines. Probably. Maybe you're like me and you need the structure in order to actually use something like this, so if that's the case then don't take my suggestions as optional, just do it. Copy my exact formatting and start today; tomorrow doesn't exist.

The intent of this is to set yourself up for success. I'd bet the reason you opted to read this is because you've tried to be confident or funny in the past, but it hasn't panned out so you're looking for other options. That's genuinely awesome—you're trying to seek out and absorb resources. If you haven't found favor in your past efforts, then there's probably a reason for it. This is me calling you out to actually follow through with positive change. Set yourself up to where you can't fail. I was in leadership training a while back and I watched a video by Eric Thomas about a mentor bringing his pupil to the ocean for his first lesson on becoming successful. The mentee had begged to be taught by this prolifically lucrative man and he finally agreed. For his initial exercise, he was thrown into the waves and his mentor shoved his head underwater so he couldn't catch a breath. After a while, he let go so that the sweet air could fill the student's lungs again. He was angry and asked his advisor why he did that, to which he replied, "When you want to succeed as bad as you want to breathe then you'll be successful." At this point ask yourself: how badly do you want self-improvement, and will you do whatever it takes to get there? Sometimes you have to go through the motions and do seemingly irrelevant or ridiculous things *Karate Kid* style to achieve what you haven't before.

Chapter Nine: The Symbiotic Relationship

Humor and confidence do a good job working in a symbiotic relationship, which is when two things work cohesively in biology. In this case, humor and confidence's symbiotic relationship is mutually beneficial, so both parties get something good out of it. A common example of mutualism in nature is between the clownfish and the sea anemone, like shown in *Finding Nemo*. The anemone is dangerous to most other fish because of the stinging cells that lay within their tentacles, which release harmful toxins to most fish. The clownfish is for some reason immune to these effects, so the anemone provides a safe home from other, more dangerous fish. If that were the end of it and the clownfish didn't harm the anemone it would be considered a commensal relationship where one benefits and the other isn't helped or harmed. The clownfish, however, also protects this sea plant. The clownfish eats many of its predators and also emits a high-frequency noise that wards others off. Not only does it scare off potentially deadly creatures of the anemone, the first also provides nutrients through its fecal matter. This is one of the most familiar examples of a symbiotic mutualistic relationship in the natural world because the two creatures, who have otherwise no interest in the other species, work cohesively to gain advantages in order to survive.

Unsurprisingly, confidence and humor do the same. This may actually come as a surprise to you if you haven't been paying attention, but let's just assume you have been with me this whole time and this isn't a shocking revelation. The way I see it, humor improves confidence and confidence fuels humor, much like the sea anemone provides safety and comfort for the little fish and the clownfish provides safety in return, as well as food. Hopefully you see the connection there; I'm not sure if I'm just grasping for straws, but stay with me, we're nearing the end anyway.

It's natural to visualize confidence as quiet, stoic, and masculine, but none of these need to apply to confidence. There's a reason why honing your humor will improve your confidence, even though humor is not often associated with quietness, stoicism, or masculinity. Our natural association of the two need to be broken down and re-evaluated because a lot of them are wrong or misplaced. I've been working to debunk the association between arrogance and confidence as well as insecurity and meekness, because they're opposites, not synonyms. It's the same type of thing for introducing the image of humor as it relates to confidence: it's probably not exactly what you'd expect. I've given a ton of reasons why this is the case, but if nothing else, it's because of the vastness of humor. Another reason is because the most confident people feel comfortable enough to laugh at themselves, which is certainly not related to quietness, stoicism, or masculinity.

Making yourself the butt of the joke is not just to appeal to the self-deprecation style of humor or because you think others don't like you so you're trying to fulfill your looking-glass self (fun fact: this scenario is another form of learned helplessness). Being silly and not taking yourself too seriously is an invitation to give yourself a pass. A pass for doing stupid or embarrassing things, which I think everyone can admit is the ideal situation; everybody wants to be spared humiliation. And this doesn't mean you're invincible to shame brought on by others, but man, does it help cushion the blow.

This goes with the thick skin advice I talked about when I was warning you what to avoid when it comes to humor. In that context, I told you not to dish it if you can't take it, but here I'm telling you to train yourself to take it even if you don't ever dish it.

    I want to make this so painfully clear: do not make fun of yourself because you think that's what others want or expect; make those jokes in good fun and without expecting a bunch of positive attention. This is a chapter full of reminders but remember you cannot control others' reactions to your humor, and that's okay. Eso si qué es. It is what it is. Fun trick: if you spell out "socks" you've pretty much got it. That tidbit is extremely helpful to me because I don't speak Spanish, as many Spanish-speakers have probably found out. By "extremely helpful" I mean remotely interesting because I can't recall a time I've ever needed to know that. I've also seen "It is what it is" being said, "Es lo qué es" in Spanish, so if that's more correct then scratch the last joke. If you're not a language fan, I'll toss in another fun fact just for the heck of it. Did you know that albino plants exist? Albino animals are already at a deep risk due to their inability to camouflage, so they typically die young in the wild, but plants are more so in trouble. Albino plants are obvious to predators, just like animals, but they're also unable to produce chlorophyll to complete the photosynthesis process independently. They can still survive if, on the off chance, they can vampire another plant's resources, but that opportunity is an extreme rarity. This symbiotic relationship would be classified as parasitic because the albino plant gets the benefit of food for survival whereas the other plant is in harm's way due to the attraction a pigment-lacking organism brings and because of the chlorophyll being stolen from their photosynthesis process.

May this fun fact please you and be used as future ice breakers to impress friends and strangers.

In the same way that healthy plants feed chlorophyll to plants with albinism, confidence feeds humor. I think we can agree that some of the boldest forms of humor are the best, which is, again, the reason dark and explicit humors can be so effective. As our self-confidence grows, so does our boldness. I say again: confidence is the cornerstone, and from it, additional wonderful traits can stem. Done right, confidence will help you gain awareness, compassion, motivation, extraversion, responsibility, and other possibly unexpected areas of maturity. And plus, becoming more confident can even help you appear more attractive; most people want to be with someone who believes in themselves. And if they prefer insecure people then you're probably dodging a bullet anyway. Think about it, do you want your partner to be confident in their abilities, decisions, and circumstance? Most people do for several reasons.

If you love somebody, you want them to succeed in everything they do, but I think at this point you and I can both agree that self-confidence can be a huge impediment to growth. After all, you'll only get as far as you think you can go. If you construct a glass ceiling for yourself, then this type of learned helplessness will perpetuate when you hit the glass ceiling, throw your hands up, and say "I knew it." You want your partner to know no bounds in terms of what they can achieve and it's on you to encourage those feelings; not to say you're responsible for their reactions, motivations, or achievements, but I certainly hope you feel inclined to celebrate with their wins, feel sad in their losses, and challenge in their in-betweens. As always, building confidence is for you, but if it helps, remember to be the kind of person you would want to date.

Similarly, just as you're not building confidence for someone else, someone else isn't responsible for building or tearing down your confidence. It's not easy building boundaries to protect yourself from the weight some people bear on our lives, but reminding yourself of your internal locus of control is important in situations when you doubt yourself due to another, whether by your own comparisons or by theirs. This can apply to other's perceptions of comedy as well. Humor shaming is something that does exist and can only be tamed by your actions. People will complain about others no matter what, especially when I'm encouraging the overlap between confidence and comedy, which is critical to deliver sometimes risky lines, even if they don't appear risky pre-delivery. Hopefully, humor shaming can largely be avoided by being wary of the audience and adjusting accordingly; but even with the audience taken into account, I'll remind you again that you can't control others' reactions.

If you've gathered nothing else from our time together, I hope you take away the impact your thoughts have on your mood, confidence, and emotions. I'm about to get cliché, so stay with me. Your mentality is your most sacred place. Only you can touch your reactions, emotions, moods, thoughts, and behaviors. It seems like we don't have control over a lot of those things, but the more we learn about the brain, the more we realize how much of an impact we can have on it, even on a conscious level. We don't need to dive into psychotherapy and concentrate on your subconscious, deepest fears, and childhood traumas to take positive steps toward a healthy mentality. You can start by practicing awareness and catching the bad thoughts that go through your head. Eventually acknowledging them will come naturally and you can work on reframing them, like we talked about in Chapter One. Reframing involves pointing out the flaws or lack of productivity in these thoughts. For example, if your thought is, "The last time I told a joke like this, it ended horribly and it was so awkward," then that might be an accurate portrayal of what happened, but it's not necessarily helpful to you unless it created a needed boundary. Sometimes our jokes don't land and it doesn't mean that joke is off-limits, it just means there might be another time and place for it. However, if the thought is, "The last time I told a joke like this, it ended horribly and it was so awkward. If I tell a joke then it'll just happen all over again," then it's considered an irrational thought because you're assuming one situation is all situations, and that's just not true. Your brain is doing its best, but it needs some help sometimes.

A common myth is that your brain is only expending about 10% of its capacity at any given moment, comparative to what your muscles exert versus its full capacity. While the latter bit about your muscles is true, brains do not only work using a tenth of their power. Your brain is constantly working at nearly full speed to ensure your body is operational; it isn't taking shortcuts to make sure you're living your best life, and neither should you. Even when asleep your brain's facilities are still functioning so you can wake up feeling rejuvenated and ready to take on a new day. Granted, I'm pretty sure there is not a single person who wakes up, stretches, and thinks, "Man, yet again I am fully rested and ready for another glorious day," because that's just not realistic, but it doesn't mean your brain isn't fighting for you. Your body is ferociously fighting to keep you going by balancing your hormones and firing neurotransmitters so the rest of your body can keep chugging along, even when you feel exhausted after a night's so-called "full" sleep.

There are times when it feels like it isn't doing its job quite right and we end up feeling depressed or anxious on some days, but some things would slip between the cracks if you had to manage the complexity of the body's normal functions. It should be noted these reactions are not at all considered to be a result of "slipping through the cracks" from your brain's perspective; it thinks it's keeping you alive by being anxious or depressed. It might feel backwards, but it's a sign your brain is being responsive to your environment, even when it feels like an impediment. Whenever you have an unideal reaction to something, whether that involves mental struggles or a simple rash, just remember that your body is doing the best it can to keep you going. When your finger gets a cut, it will slightly swell and redden. Although annoying, this is because your body's little ambulance cells are rushing to its aid; some might refer to them as white blood cells which is also fine, I suppose. They tape off the area to make sure it's isolated and start working tirelessly to mend the wound—which you caused, for the record. To us, it's an inconvenient process at best and painful at worst. Self-esteem needs to be treated the same. It's worth it to go through the pains of identifying, isolating, and rebuilding the parts that are lacking. Sometimes it gets confused because it thinks there are foreign cells and it attacks them even though they're normal cells and boom—you've got an autoimmune disease. But give yourself a break, your body shouldn't be hated on just because it's learned the best way to survive up to this point, and neither should you.

You wouldn't blame someone else for being indecisive if you knew their parents were incredibly controlling and they left straight for the military, a place where nothing is their choice. It only makes sense that they would leave those circumstances as someone who isn't sure of their own decisions, especially since they've been told what to do for the last two or more decades. Work to control what you can but give yourself grace for what you can't; at the foundation, you're a product of your environment, for better or for worse. The age-old argument of nature versus nurture comes into play here. Do you have an undeviating choice in how you've developed, including your personality, or are you merely an active spectator in your own life? This is a topic left to the philosophers, but I'll try the thought on for size to get the gears in your brain moving and considering different perspectives. And honestly, the more I contribute to you becoming educationally well-rounded through my spewing of random cultural, psychological, philosophical, and biological facts, the more equipped you'll feel. I don't know a whole lot, as you can see, but I try to use examples from real life to teach a little about nature and a lot about humans; well, what I know anyway. These tangents help me share what I know so you can share it someday, too. It's particularly useful for conversation starters and sounding smarter than you are. Anyway, back to philosophical arguments.

There are some theories that believe you have absolutely no free will, both can be argued from non-secular and secular perspectives. Religious folks might claim there's no free will because of predestination, which is arguably represented and suggested throughout the Judeo-Christian's Holy Bible. Nonsecular people might say there's no free will because we're all at the mercy of our environment; we have moods that impact our thoughts and feelings and we're essentially put in a situation to decide based on these factors.

Essentially these factors pigeonhole us into choosing things that have already been assumed. It feels like we're in control, but we're not, according to these theories. I'm not here to propose a theological or philosophical debate, people have been butting heads about this topic for centuries, but needless to say, the debate is alive and well. So maybe it's appropriate to consider: do you have control or are you merely a pawn? It's hard to say, but what's the alternative, do nothing? Shrug and say, "This is how it's meant to be"? I don't think that's the case. Even if our decisions were premeditated somehow, I think we still have a responsibility to do right by ourselves and others the best we know-how. The cerebral theories almost don't matter; the debate may be fiery to prove who's right and who's wrong, but you still have to experience the day regardless.

I think that you owe something to yourself, whether free will exists or not. You owe it to yourself because however you were created, for whatever purpose, it wasn't an accident. And if it was an accident, we're all accidents, so that doesn't mean you're exempt. Your value is indicative of the fact that you're here, breathing and reading this. Your desire to be better and feel better further proves my point; you have something to offer to the world, no matter how many things seem to be fighting you, even when it's your own mental struggles. I maintain the firm belief that people should seek mental health treatment just as they would for physical health. I have already mentioned this, but I want to reiterate that you should check in with a mental health professional every six to twelve months, just like you get check-ups for physicals. Taking care of yourself is an intentional investment that you should not address superficially.

Chapter Ten: What We Learned

Well, we've reached the end. And if you haven't figured that out by the final chapter's title then, well, life's going to be rough, pal. But even if it's rough hopefully you can feel confident in yourself regardless because, again, at the end of the day, my opinion doesn't matter and, neither do others' opinions. I'm not going to talk about "all the fun we've had" because that feels pretty cringey and cheesy, but I will once again thank you for being here. Maybe you've flipped to the last chapter to see if this is all worth it and that's okay too, but if you've made it through every in between then hopefully you feel self-gratitude for getting through it. I know I haven't been the easiest to read throughout, but my hope is that you've picked up valuable information.

If you forget everything as soon as you read or hear something, like me, you're in luck. I know what it's like to have read a full book and forgotten just about everything, so let me take you through a recap. This book is split into three sections: Part I: Confidence, Part II: Humor, and Part III: Applying Both. Part I emphasized the importance of how you perceive yourself and how it can have an impact on your self-confidence. We know from each section that it's difficult to get anything done if you aren't aware of it in the first place, and it becomes a debatably worse issue if the things you're aware of simply aren't true, particularly information gathered from your presumption of other people's perception. Your looking-glass self is how you predict others view you, and it's typically used against yourself by assuming the worst. Being aware of the looking-glass self and adjusting the presumptions that come with it are important parts of learning to focus on self-growth. Remind yourself that other people have their attention on themselves and, most of the time, they couldn't be concerned with the ongoings of those around them. Sometimes being unaware of what people are thinking about you can be annoying, but if you let it, it can be quite comforting.

An absolutely ground-breaking, life-changing concept is positive thinking, which comes with thinking less negatively and decreasing complaints. It's hard to prevent yourself from being negative because taking habits out is always more difficult than adding them in, so it becomes easier as you replace it with the positive thoughts instead. Positive thinking is referenced and re-referenced countless times in all three parts because it can reframe the way you perceive yourself, including how you perceive your own humor. Go back and review Chapter One: Awareness to revisit tips on how to apply positive thinking more naturally and frequently. Chapter Two: Application offers specific advice for how to actively enhance confidence. Body language is a huge part of training your brain to feel, and eventually be, confident. This goes well with observing confident people: how do they act and what's their body language like? I can already tell you their posture is probably upright, and their eyes will likely appear focused, even if it's on nothing specific. If your chin is glued to your chest and your eyes stray to the ground or your phone, it won't convey confidence. These suggestions aren't definite "no"s—you can look at your phone in public—but if you want to look and feel confident when you go out, these will certainly help. It's a learning curve because you might feel stupid at first but give it your best shot and see what happens. And of course, a good general rule of thumb is to come prepared. You can typically guess what the situation will be like before you get there, so think of ways to anticipate needs or opportunities and strategize accordingly. Coming prepared as it relates to confidence means showing up to an event with a joke, talent, or story in your back pocket. Even if you're not much of a performer or extravert, this is useful advice for a small group or for interpersonal conversations. You may not whip out dance moves or a full rap if it's one-on-one, but stories can be told in front of millions or one, and that flexibility is the great thing about planning ahead.

And as we learned in Chapter Three, coming prepared is not the only way to equip yourself for success. In this chapter, I encourage you to dig into your insecurities to help identify why you might be lacking self-confidence and how we can debunk destructive, irrational thoughts through the basics of Cognitive Behavior Therapy (CBT). I also discussed "happiness investments," which are decisions that may be uncomfortable in the moment, but they come with a promising return of enjoyment later on. This could involve going back to school for a degree in the field you've been interested in or starting an exercise routine or pouring additional time into your relationships. These investments should contribute to feelings of satisfaction and confidence. Improving competence in specific, practical skills of interest is also a great way to invest your time and energy into yourself. This is also beneficial because you're maintaining productivity in the meantime, which is a necessary requirement for some busy adults. Despite the busyness we might feel pressured to uphold, one significant message in this section reminds you that nothing is good in excess; even if you commit yourself to growth through these measures, it's important to take them in moderation to nurture a sustainable, long-lasting improvement. Sometimes the best reward is rest. If need be, you can consider this a happiness investment too, because sometimes you miss out on doing something fun or getting something done in order to squeeze rest into your schedule.

Part II focused on absorbing, embodying, and anticipating opportunities for humor. We reviewed a few different types of humor, especially common ones you might come across in a typical day, such as dry humor, word play, epigrammatic, dark humor, and so forth. It's important to consider what part humor plays in our lives, which is why we talked a bit about how it relates to other cultures. And speaking of paying attention to other cultures, another bit of wisdom is to look for humor wherever you go, because noticing it other places will continually plant and water a seed in your brain of how humor can fit in situations you might not have noticed before. It can also assist with identifying your own style of humor, especially when taking inspiration from comedians, who have established their comedic voice.

I also talked about warnings of what not to do or what to consider when attempting to be funny. Things like bullying, harassment, passive aggression, poor delivery, pandering, and breaking social rules were all mentioned in a description of what not to do. This is a broad list that doesn't exclusively apply to a general group of occasions, so it might be beneficial to go back and give yourself a refresher on this one. More than I, others may advise limiting yourself when using brash forms of humor, but my basic advice involves following along your own best judgment; if you have used your best judgment in the past and bad things happened anyway, then maybe it's appropriate to use someone else's best judgment by asking yourself what they would do in your situation. Alternatively, you can just, you know, ask someone with better judgment for their opinion on the situation—that works, too.

In Chapter Six: Planning Ahead, we discussed, well, the title: planning ahead. As I've mentioned, I think about approximately 80% of my jokes prior to the moment. Anticipating and planning for these specific situations allows for them to appear spontaneous and well-spoken to the audience but provides confidence and concision for your own benefit, it's the best of both worlds. However, I use awareness as a tool for my style of humor so I might point out that I planned the joke in advance to continue my attempt at being funny. For example, my spouse and I were at a coffee shop and we were joking with our favorite barista that I wasn't wearing my wedding ring: how were others supposed to know I'm off-limits to potential suitors? It became a trend back-to-back because apparently, I forget to put it on after showers, so I go full days without wearing it. One day I decided to wear two rings to make a joke of the situation, claiming that no one can't *not* know I'm married. I boasted the two rings, which were randomly chosen and not complimentary by the way, the next time we ran into the same barista at our next visit to the coffee shop. We laughed about it briefly and I admitted that I planned this joke ahead of time and I wore it all day in anticipation. I like to include these bits of self-awareness because it makes fun of myself in silly ways and highlights the fact that I'm aware of just how ridiculous my jokes can be, it's kind of my go-to. I'd consider it a backhanded compliment to myself because on one hand, I'm delivering a hopefully funny joke, but on the other hand, I'm pointing out something I did wrong, odd, or something that people don't often admit.

Another example of this type of humor involves my incredible lack of attention. A coworker and I often collaborate and problem solve, but when she's explaining an issue, I find my consciousness wandering off to dinner later tonight or a funny video I saw the day before, so halfway through her explanation I realize I'll have no context to weigh in when we get to the problem solving part of the conversation. If we were less friendly or we had established more of a professional tone, I would have probably said something along the lines of, "Would you mind repeating the first bit, I was reviewing our most recent messages and I seemed to have missed what you said," or "Okay, so you said [last bit of information I heard], but remind me, how did you get there again?" or perhaps some other way that's a more natural way to get her to repeat the story. Instead, I say, "I'm so very sorry. I was not paying attention whatsoever; can you start over?" She knows me and is forgiving of my absentmindedness, so we are able to laugh about it. It's hard to miss tone when reading things, so perhaps the light-heartedness of the circumstance doesn't translate well, but she's a good sport so it's always funny to us.

I give examples for this type of humor because it's difficult to explain, which is why I did not include it in the list in Chapter Four's description of humors. Humor is extremely dynamic and not something you can suddenly pick up from reading a book, it's something you've got to experience and practice in advance. I can give you tips and tricks all day, but unless you expose yourself to real life humor, I'm not exactly sure how much reading will help. Figure out what style you connect with by watching someone else do it and it'll be easier to translate it to your normal life instead of reading some words and going from there. Imagine circumstances where someone with dry humor, like me, would say something like those examples above: Do you find them funny? Try to wait until you get one of these in the wild to truly determine, especially since my dry humor does not look like everyone else's, particularly if I'm limited in my communication through text. Everybody's style is different, even when it's in the same category, which is why making humor your own is so important.

In the beginning of Part III, we reviewed the purpose of humor and confidence. Why do we, as humans, feel compelled to romanticize these traits, and are they necessary for our survival in today's times? It's easily argued amongst professionals that sometimes, yes, it was considered life or death to be likeable before technology became a social crutch, but now it's easier to get by without these qualities. But you haven't come this far into this book because you're on the cusp of death after being ostracized by society and you're forced to find a way to make amends by becoming funny and self-assured. You're reading this because you already know the value of these traits, and Chapter Seven goes over the most likely reasons we feel the desire to obtain them. The Purpose discusses viewpoints by known evolutionist Charles Darwin and psychologist Sigmund Freud, who both hypothesize the role humor plays in our lives. Confidence is also viewed under a microscope as we talk about how social success and natural selection play a part. CBT is brought up again and it's discussed the impact confidence has on one's psychology.

Chapter Eight challenges your awareness, as the title indicates. I think it can be agreed upon at this point that awareness is the crux of self-improvement, so in that chapter, I talk about how you can be intentional with being aware and how that can apply to your progress. This can be gathered from asking people you know and trust how they perceive you, particularly in relation to your humor and confidence. It's best if you check in semi-regularly with your sources to draw a better conceptualization of your progress. If you feel really wild you can create a basic survey for your friends to anonymously complete, but I get that it's a bit much; that's not lost on me.

You can also be somewhat self-reliant in taking note of your improvement by journaling and maintaining a behavior log, which can track mood, confidence, humor, weather, exercise, or whatever else you find relevant. Noticing external factors that might affect your confidence or humor in a day can be helpful in better understanding how to let certain things roll off your back or how to balance it out. If you notice you're less confident during cloudy days, maybe pick out an outfit that makes you look really good or pick up coffee before work to put you in a better mood. You can start to counteract these external factors before they have any real impact as you gain more awareness for how things affect you. You don't necessarily need tangible, measurable data to show how much you've grown, but it really helps. Seeing this type of growth is one of the best ways to sustain and expand the strides you've made. Imagine wanting to lose weight, so you start exercising and eating healthy, but you can't check your weight or look at your body along the way. It would get disheartening pretty quickly, wouldn't it? This is no different. Set goals, keep some kind of record, and re-evaluate through the process and as you see change.

Chapter Nine was quite literally the previous chapter, so I hope you haven't forgotten what we discussed already. I'll still talk about it because the inconsistency of excluding a full chapter in this summary breakdown just because it's too recent would drive me bonkers. And plus, I already conceded that this section is partially for those who skip to the end and I'm not about to let you all down now. The Symbiotic Relationship reviewed examples in nature of creatures experiencing a mutualistic, communalistic, and parasitic relationship. Mutualism refers to when two separate species gain benefits from each other, communalism is one animal benefitting but the other is mostly unharmed, and parasitic is one creature taking advantage of another to where it harms the second party. If you did happen to skip this chapter, that's fine, but as someone who is fascinated with information about nature, I'd urge you to check it out to learn a bit about wildlife before I tie it back with the main purpose, which follows.

Humor and confidence are considered to be mutualistic because they help each other out by promoting one another. As you receive satisfaction and approval from your humor, it helps cultivate self-confidence. As you build confidence, you start to feel comfortable telling jokes more frequently and trying different types that you might've felt were too risky. These two components are cyclical in nature, and, in some ways, can help curb one another if necessary. If you get out of control with your humor and start to become overly self-important as a result, ego will balance itself out as social rejection likely arrives. As I said, social perception isn't all that, but I'm guessing you wouldn't want the social consequences being too big-headed for your own good. Humility and silliness are great anchors to make sure you don't get to the point of judgment or exclusion. The point is for the two to work together for the positive good and to balance out one another.

I hope I haven't just built a monster by equipping you with all this knowledge. If you already feel yourself transforming into an egotistical wreck, the least you can do is pretend you didn't get these ideas from me. My ultimate advice is for you to get it together, and that's on the record. If nothing else, I hope you've enjoyed the ride from confidence to humor and using them both. But, more importantly, I also hope you've gotten more insightful, aware, and motivated after reading this. I hope you walk away and feel empowered to improve your self-confidence and your humor, knowing that it can change your life if you let it. I appreciate you being here and finishing with me. I've only heard this in passive-aggressive or stiff, professional contexts, but please know I mean this in all sincerity from the bottom of my heart: best of luck to you.

www.ingramcontent.com/pod-product-compliance
Lightning Source LLC
Chambersburg PA
CBHW071455070526
44578CB00001B/342